Adobe

Photoshop

Elements Bible

The Essential Handbook for Visual Creators

CARLOS F. MORGAN

TABLE OF CONTENTS

Preface..**12**

  Who This Book Is For.. 12

      For Beginners.. 13

      For Intermediate Creators...13

      For Freelancers and Business Users..13

      For Non-Designers..13

  What's New in 2025: Updated Features and Interface Changes.............14

      Automated Correction Tools..14

      Layer Management Improvements...14

      Improved Text Tool Behaviors..14

      Cloud Syncing Adjustments..15

      Export Settings and Output Formats...15

  Navigating This Handbook Efficiently... 15

      Use the Table of Contents Like a Toolbox....................................15

      Follow the Workflow Tips.. 16

      Skip What Doesn't Apply.. 16

      Bookmark the Appendices.. 16

Chapter 1...**18**

System Requirements, Installation, and Configuration.......................**18**

  What You Need for Peak Performance..18

      Minimum vs. Practical Requirements..18

          Suggested Practical Specifications:.......................................19

      Hardware Considerations.. 19

      Software Environment..19

  Choosing Between the Organizer and Editor.. 20

      Understanding Their Roles... 20

          The Organizer:... 20

          The Editor:... 20

      When to Use Each One... 21

  Customizing Your Workspace for Speed & Efficiency.............................. 21

      Selecting the Right Mode..21

      Reorganizing Panels and Tools.. 22

      Customizing Tool Settings..22

      Keyboard Shortcuts and Workflow Enhancers............................. 23

Chapter 2...**24**

Understanding the Interface in 2025...**24**

  Home Screen Deep Dive... 24

      Layout Overview... 24

      Customizing the Home Experience...25

Workspace Modes: Quick, Guided, Expert...25
   Quick Mode...26
      Ideal For:..26
   Guided Mode..26
      Best Suited For:...26
   Expert Mode...27
      Built For:..27
Navigating Panels, Tools, and Contextual Menus..27
   Toolbar...27
   Options Bar...28
   Panels..28
   Contextual Menus..28
Touch-Enabled Devices and Interface Shortcuts..29
   Touch Support Features..29
   Stylus Optimization...29
   Keyboard Shortcuts That Boost Efficiency..29

Chapter 3..**31**
File Management & Project Workflow...**31**
Smart File Naming, Version Control, and Organization.......................................31
   File Naming Best Practices...31
   Version Control Without Confusion..32
   Folder Structure That Supports Workflow...32
Working with RAW, JPEG, PSD, PNG, and TIFF..33
   RAW...33
   JPEG..34
   PSD..34
   PNG..34
   TIFF..35
Non-Destructive Editing Principles..35
   Techniques That Preserve Image Integrity...35
      Use Adjustment Layers...35
      Duplicate the Base Layer..36
      Use Layer Masks Instead of Erasing..36
      Convert to Smart Objects..36
      Save Progressive Versions..36
Exporting: Web vs Print-Ready Assets..36
   For Web or Screen Display...36
   For Print...37

Chapter 4..**39**
Brushes, Selections, and Layers – The Holy Trinity..**39**
Understanding Layer Logic..39

Pixel Layers...39

Adjustment Layers..40

Text Layers..40

Smart Layers..41

Selections: Lasso, Quick, Object, and Refine Edge Techniques..................41

Lasso Tools: Precision and Freeform Control.......................................41

Freehand Lasso...41

Polygonal Lasso..41

Magnetic Lasso...42

Quick Selection Tool: Speed Meets Intelligence...................................42

Object Selection: Modern Automation..42

Refine Edge and Masking Techniques..43

Brush Mastery: Custom Brushes, Opacity Flow, and Blending Modes..................43

Creating and Managing Custom Brushes...43

Opacity and Flow: The Difference Explained..44

Blending Modes: How Layers Interact..45

Chapter 5...**46**

The Power of Adjustment Layers and Filters..**46**

Using Brightness/Contrast, Levels, and Curves Like a Technician................46

Brightness/Contrast: The Blunt Yet Useful Tool....................................46

Levels: Targeted Control Over Tonal Range...47

Curves: The Advanced Technician's Playground....................................47

Color Correction Fundamentals..48

Neutralizing Color Casts..48

Skin Tone Correction..49

Saturation and Vibrance...49

Filter Gallery vs Smart Filters – What Works Where?...............................50

Filter Gallery: Experimental and Aesthetic Modifiers..............................50

Smart Filters: Reversible and Non-Destructive.....................................50

Dodging, Burning, and Sharpening Without Overdoing It............................51

Dodging: Lightening Specific Areas..51

Burning: Darkening Areas for Depth..51

Sharpening: Enhancing Texture, Not Noise..52

Chapter 6...**53**

Retouching and Restoration...**53**

Clone Stamp vs Healing Brush vs Content-Aware...................................53

Clone Stamp: Full Manual Control..53

Healing Brush: Texture + Tone Integration...54

Content-Aware Fill: Letting the Software Predict....................................54

Fixing Old Photos: Dust, Tears, and Fading...55

Removing Dust and Scratches...55

Repairing Tears and Creases...56

Addressing Fading and Discoloration..56

Smoothing Skin Without Losing Texture..57

Frequency Separation: Texture vs Tone...57

Simpler Method: Low-Flow Healing + Blur...58

Removing Objects Cleanly (People, Wires, Blemishes)...58

Removing People from Backgrounds..58

Removing Wires and Lines...59

Removing Blemishes or Minor Distractions..59

Chapter 7..62

Compositing Magic – From Cutouts to Concept Art..62

Background Replacements Done Right...62

Step 1: Precise Subject Extraction...63

Step 2: Choose a Matching Background...63

Step 3: Blending with Adjustments...64

Matching Light, Color, and Perspective..64

Matching Light Direction and Quality..64

Matching Color Temperature..65

Matching Perspective...65

Layer Masks vs Clipping Masks...66

Layer Masks: Non-Destructive Visibility Control..66

Clipping Masks: Targeted Adjustments..66

Creating Seamless Multi-Image Blends..67

Step-by-Step Guide to Seamless Blending..67

Chapter 8..70

Typography, Design, and Graphic Layouts...70

Working with Text Tools and Type Layers...70

Creating and Editing Type Layers..70

Converting Text to Shapes or Paths...71

Text Effects: Glow, Warp, and Stroke..72

Outer Glow and Drop Shadow..72

Stroke (Outline)..73

Warping Text..73

Creating Social Media Banners, Flyers, and Mockups...73

Social Media Banners...74

Flyer and Poster Design...74

Mockup Creation..75

Layout Best Practices for Web & Print..75

Web Layouts...75

Print Layouts...76

Chapter 9..78

Guided Edits That Don't Look Cheesy..**78**

    Making the Most of Built-In Tools...78

        Understanding Guided Edits..78

        How to Keep Guided Edits Looking Tasteful..79

    Stylized Effects: Double Exposure, Pop Art, and Depth-of-Field Illusions............80

        Double Exposure...80

        Pop Art Treatment..80

        Depth-of-Field Simulations..81

    Cinemagraphs, Collages, and Scroll-Stopping Visuals.....................................82

        Cinemagraphs: Controlled Motion in Still Frames....................................82

        Collage Work Without Chaos..83

        Scroll-Stopping Visuals...83

Chapter 10..**85**

Creative Projects to Build Your Portfolio..**85**

    Photo Diary Layouts...85

        Purpose..85

        How to Build a Photo Diary Layout...86

        Tips for Refinement..87

    Magazine-Style Portrait Retouches..87

        Purpose..87

        Building the Project..88

        Final Layout...88

    Product Mockups for Digital Shops and Print-on-Demand.................................89

        Purpose..89

        How to Create Product Mockups..89

        Product Categories to Showcase..90

    Concept Posters Using Layer Stacking...90

        Purpose..90

        How to Construct a Concept Poster..91

        Poster Composition Guidelines..92

Chapter 11..**94**

Custom Presets, Actions, and Batch Editing...**94**

    Setting Up Presets for Repetitive Tasks...94

        What Presets Can Control...95

        Practical Uses of Custom Presets..95

        How to Create and Save Your Own Presets...95

    Creating and Recording Actions in Elements...96

        What Can Be Recorded in an Action..96

        Steps to Record an Action (Compatible Editors).......................................96

        Tips for Building Better Actions...97

    Batch Resizing, Watermarking, and Auto-Touch-Up Scripts.............................97

Batch Resizing...98

Batch Watermarking..98

Auto-Touch-Up Scripts...99

Keeping Things Organized..100

Folder Naming...100

Backing Up Presets and Actions...100

Chapter 12...**102**

Color Grading Like a Filmmaker...**102**

Color Lookup Tables (LUTs) in Elements..102

What Are LUTs?..102

How LUTs Work in Photo Editors...103

Common LUT Formats..103

Where to Source Free and Legal LUTs..103

How to Apply LUTs in Common Editors...103

Cinematic Grading Techniques...104

Color Psychology and Storytelling..104

Basic Grading Layers to Work With..105

Building a Film-Like Grade from Scratch...105

Creating Your Own Look Presets...106

How to Save Custom Looks...106

Tips for Better Grading Presets..106

Key Considerations for Visual Consistency...107

Chapter 13...**108**

Advanced Selections, Channels, and Blend Strategies..**108**

Hair Selections, Glass, and Translucent Objects...108

Why These Elements Are Difficult..108

Techniques for Isolating Hair...109

Handling Glass and Semi-Transparent Surfaces..109

Using Blend Modes with Purpose..110

Key Blend Modes and When to Use Them..110

Multiply..110

Screen...110

Overlay..111

Soft Light..111

Color..111

Luminosity...111

Tips for Clean Blending..112

Multi-Channel Compositing Techniques...112

Understanding the Channel Structure...112

Isolating Detail Through Channels..113

Combining Multiple Channels for Special Effects...113

Practical Application Scenarios..114
    Isolating a Person from a Busy Background...............................114
    Adding a Glass Object into a Scene.......................................114
Chapter 14...**116**
Working with Clients and Deliverables.......................................**116**
    Preparing Print-Ready Files: Bleed, CMYK, and Sizing....................116
        What Makes a File "Print-Ready"?....................................116
        Bleed and Trim Zones..116
        CMYK vs. RGB..117
        Resizing Without Losing Quality....................................118
    Understanding DPI, Resolution, and Export Formats.......................118
        DPI vs. PPI: Know the Difference....................................118
        Resolution Tips for Print Projects.................................119
        Choosing the Right File Format.....................................119
    How to Package and Deliver Files Like a Pro.............................120
        Organizing Final Files..120
        Packaging for Print Production......................................121
        Delivering Files to Clients..122
    Tips for Communicating with Clients.....................................122
Chapter 15...**124**
Building a Side Hustle with Your Skills....................................**124**
    Selling Templates, Presets, and Digital Art.............................124
        Why Digital Products Are a Smart Choice.............................124
        Types of Digital Products You Can Sell..............................124
            Templates...124
            Presets...125
            Digital Art...125
        Platforms to Sell Your Work...125
            Examples of Distribution Methods:...............................126
        How to Make Your Products Stand Out.................................126
    Freelancing for Small Businesses and Creators...........................127
        Why Target Small Businesses?.......................................127
        Services You Can Offer..127
        Where to Find Clients (Without Platform Name-Dropping)..............127
        Structuring Your Freelance Offers...................................128
    Licensing Your Work and Copyright Tips..................................128
        Understanding Copyright Basics......................................128
        Types of Licensing..129
            Personal Use License..129
            Commercial Use License..129
            Exclusive vs. Non-Exclusive.....................................129

How to Protect Your Work...129

Drafting Simple Licensing Agreements...130

Tips for Growing Your Side Hustle Sustainably.. 130

Appendices & Bonus Resources..**132**

Appendix A: Keyboard Shortcuts Cheat Sheet (2025 Edition)........................... 132

General Workflow Shortcuts... 132

Selection and Navigation... 133

Layer and Object Controls... 133

Appendix B: Free Online Assets and Brush Repositories.................................. 133

Open License Image Resources...134

Free Brush Libraries.. 134

Icons and Vector Files...134

Appendix C: Troubleshooting Guide for Crashes, Lag, and Errors...................135

Crashes on Launch..135

Sluggish Performance or Lag.. 135

Freezes When Exporting.. 136

Appendix D: Legal Use of Stock Images and AI-Generated Content................. 136

Stock Image Usage Rules.. 136

AI-Generated Content Guidelines...137

Appendix E: How to Stay Updated Without Relearning Everything....................137

Use Official Product Documentation... 137

Subscribe to Non-Commercial Learning Platforms...138

Watch Software Update Videos.. 138

Don't Update Mid-Project... 138

Keep a "What Changed" Log.. 138

Preface

The purpose of this book is practical: to help digital creators, designers, freelancers, and hobbyists make the most of their time and talent. Whether you're just starting or refining your current process, this handbook is intended to serve as a useful companion throughout your creative journey. The tools and techniques explored here are not tied to a specific brand or platform. Instead, they reflect universally accessible methods that align with professional workflows and industry expectations.

This handbook has been shaped with one primary goal in mind—to reduce confusion and increase productivity. Many creative resources are either too vague or too bloated, stuffed with terminology that doesn't connect to everyday problems. What you'll find here are straightforward explanations, clear examples, and reliable methods built on free and open-source knowledge. No expensive add-ons. No secret paywalls. Just direct, applicable skills.

Over the past year, digital tools have changed in subtle but important ways. Some interface designs have shifted. Certain features have been removed, while others have become automated. For someone who just wants to create without reading through corporate blogs or attending paid webinars, the confusion can be frustrating. This book filters out the noise, giving you only what matters.

Who This Book Is For

This handbook is written with clarity and flexibility in mind, to be useful across a wide range of user profiles. You don't need formal training or expensive hardware to apply the concepts discussed here. If you can access a free or affordable design tool, and you're willing to apply some structure to your creative sessions, you already have everything required.

For Beginners

If you're new to creative software, this book can be your initial reference. You'll find foundational explanations, step-by-step walkthroughs, and vocabulary broken down into plain terms. Instead of technical jargon, you'll get terminology explained in a way that connects to real-world tasks—editing photos, preparing visuals for a client, making social media assets, or creating your own personal portfolio.

For Intermediate Creators

For those with some experience, the guide provides structure and direction to your workflow. You may already know how to use the basic tools, but refining your process and avoiding unnecessary friction is where this book becomes most valuable. It's designed to prevent wasted time on trial and error or confusion from cluttered software changes.

For Freelancers and Business Users

If you're producing content for others—whether as a side gig or a full-time freelancer—there are chapters aimed specifically at streamlining your client workflow, setting up reusable templates, managing file exports, and avoiding legal missteps with images and AI content.

For Non-Designers

Even if you don't consider yourself a designer, but you manage content, coordinate marketing, or run a small business, you'll find tools here that can help you reduce your dependency on external services. You don't have to learn a full graphic suite to crop an image correctly or to export a clean banner. You just need the right instructions, at the right time.

What's New in 2025: Updated Features and Interface Changes

Each year brings subtle but impactful updates across the most commonly used creative tools. These are not always obvious unless you follow developer notes, which most users don't have the time or interest to read. Below is a summary of changes observed across several platforms based on publicly shared, non-branded information.

Automated Correction Tools

In 2025, many free and low-cost creative platforms have introduced expanded "auto-adjust" tools. These functions can now correct lighting, fix color balance, or sharpen images without manual input. While convenient, these features often sacrifice control for speed. In the handbook, you'll find side-by-side comparisons between manual and automated workflows, so you can choose what suits your project.

Layer Management Improvements

Layer organization has seen improvements, including collapsible grouping and color-coded labels in several programs. For creators working on large files, this change reduces visual clutter and makes editing faster. This book outlines a naming convention method that allows for consistent file management, even when switching between software.

Improved Text Tool Behaviors

Text editing across many free tools has become more intuitive, with fewer bugs and more consistent spacing between fonts and line breaks. The updated guide includes tips for formatting titles, subtitles, and paragraph content that maintain visual consistency across screen sizes.

Cloud Syncing Adjustments

Free-tier users of several cloud-based platforms have reported storage limits being reduced or altered. This handbook now includes a section on exporting and organizing your files offline to avoid sync interruptions or unexpected deletion.

Export Settings and Output Formats

Many platforms have altered default export behaviors, often prioritizing web-optimized file types over traditional print-ready formats. This can be frustrating for anyone trying to print a high-resolution image or deliver clean files to a client. This edition includes updated guidelines for choosing the correct format and resolution for your intended use.

Navigating This Handbook Efficiently

This book has been written in modular sections. You do not need to read it in a strict order. You can begin with the chapter that solves your immediate concern—whether it's setting up a custom workspace, fixing a slow system, or learning how to price your freelance work.

Each chapter includes clear headings, subheadings, and specific use-case scenarios. You'll also find checklists and examples where applicable. Here's how to move through the content with purpose:

Use the Table of Contents Like a Toolbox

Instead of reading straight through, look at the chapter list as a set of tools. Choose the problem you're dealing with, then go directly to that section. Whether it's a file export issue or understanding licensing terms, the information is organized to support quick reference.

Follow the Workflow Tips

At the end of several chapters, you'll find short workflow examples—these are mini-guides designed to show how a tool or feature is used within a project. They're not case studies. They're immediate applications you can replicate with your own assets.

Skip What Doesn't Apply

This book covers a wide skill range. You may not need every tip. Feel free to ignore the sections that don't apply to your current situation. It's built to be a long-term reference, not a tutorial series with prerequisites.

Bookmark the Appendices

The appendices contain fast-access content like shortcut keys, brush repositories, and legal reference notes. These are frequently updated and structured to answer quick questions during a project rather than explain concepts in depth.

Part I
Getting Set Up Like a Pro

Chapter 1

System Requirements, Installation, and Configuration

The first step in any productive editing journey begins long before a single image is touched. It's rooted in ensuring your system is up to the task, understanding the tool's structure, and configuring the environment in a way that supports creative momentum. This chapter focuses on building a strong technical foundation, so performance isn't a barrier to productivity.

What You Need for Peak Performance

Minimum vs. Practical Requirements

While most software developers offer a set of baseline requirements, those are rarely ideal for professional work. Editing software typically includes both a media organizer and an image editor, each demanding varying levels of power depending on your intended workload.

For smooth performance, a device should exceed minimum specifications. Tasks such as applying adjustment layers, blending multiple images, or running batch edits benefit heavily from faster processing and more memory. Here's a comparison of what's often acceptable versus what's actually efficient.

Suggested Practical Specifications:

- **Processor**: Quad-core (3.0 GHz or faster)

- **RAM**: 16 GB or higher

- **Storage**: SSD with at least 20 GB of free space

- **Graphics**: Dedicated GPU with 2GB VRAM (OpenGL support enabled)

- **Display**: 1920 x 1080 resolution or higher

- **Operating System**: Latest version of Windows 11 or macOS Monterey and above

- **Internet**: Required for installation, updates, and content libraries

Hardware Considerations

An older system with limited RAM or traditional hard drives can still run editing tools, but performance will suffer under pressure. Long loading times, laggy brush strokes, and sluggish responsiveness when navigating layers are all common symptoms. Investing in an SSD alone can cut load times in half and reduce autosave interruptions.

A calibrated monitor isn't mandatory but makes a significant difference when color accuracy is important. Visual projects intended for print or professional display should always be reviewed on a color-accurate screen.

Software Environment

Background applications can sap performance without offering any value. Before launching your editing tool, close any high-memory applications, pause unnecessary system updates, and disable antivirus scanning temporarily (only if safe to do so). This allows your software to access system resources without interference.

Choosing Between the Organizer and Editor

Understanding Their Roles

The tool you're using is split into two distinct functions: one for managing media, and another for editing. These are often referred to as the organizer and the editor. While both live within the same installation, they serve different purposes.

The Organizer:

- Acts as a visual media library

- Offers keyword tagging, face recognition, and automatic sorting

- Helps in locating assets quickly when working with hundreds of files

- Includes basic correction tools such as red-eye removal and auto enhancements

The Editor:

- Designed for pixel-level changes and creative manipulation

- Offers three modes: fast edits, guided assistance, and manual expert control

- Includes layer management, masking tools, and detailed retouching options

- Supports effects, text, and design layouts

When to Use Each One

The organizer is ideal for large projects that involve curating dozens or hundreds of images. If you're working on a wedding album, a stock image collection, or a long-term project, the organizer helps sort and manage your files with efficiency.

On the other hand, the editor should be the default for anyone performing image corrections, enhancements, layout designs, or anything requiring brushwork or fine selections. If you're exporting for clients or creating digital assets, the editor is non-negotiable.

Many users skip the organizer entirely and manage their files manually via system folders. This works well for photographers or designers who already have a strong file management habit. However, those new to sorting visual media might benefit from the extra structure provided.

Customizing Your Workspace for Speed & Efficiency

A one-size-fits-all approach rarely works when editing visuals. Different projects require different tools. The editing interface can be adjusted in subtle but powerful ways to make your workflow more efficient.

Selecting the Right Mode

Upon launch, the editor usually offers three modes:

- **Quick**: For basic edits with sliders and minimal tools

- **Guided**: Offers step-by-step instructions for common tasks

- **Expert**: Full control over layers, brushes, selections, and advanced tools

Switching between modes can be done from the top interface bar. Most professionals work in Expert mode, where all editing tools are accessible.

Reorganizing Panels and Tools

Panels such as **Layers**, **Effects**, **History**, and **Navigator** can be moved, resized, or minimized to suit your workflow. If you frequently switch between layer adjustments and effects, placing both side-by-side increases your editing speed.

To avoid clutter, keep only essential panels visible. Extra windows can be opened from the "Window" dropdown menu.

It's also helpful to dock your most-used tools in a consistent arrangement. For example:

- Keep the Layers panel docked on the right

- Place the History panel just below it

- Keep Effects and Adjustments on the left side

This symmetrical layout allows your eyes to locate controls faster, improving hand-eye coordination during edits.

Customizing Tool Settings

Every tool has a settings bar, usually positioned at the top once the tool is selected. Adjusting default brush size, feather strength, opacity, and hardness ahead of time prevents constant back-and-forth adjustments.

For tools like the clone stamp, healing brush, or selection tools, saving preferred settings as defaults can shave hours off your weekly workflow.

Keyboard Shortcuts and Workflow Enhancers

Speed in editing is closely tied to muscle memory. Learning just a handful of shortcut keys can double your productivity.

Here are five to remember early:

- **Ctrl/Cmd + Z** – Undo

- **Ctrl/Cmd + J** – Duplicate Layer

- **[and]** – Increase/decrease brush size

- **Spacebar + Click** – Temporary hand tool to move around the canvas

- **Ctrl/Cmd + 0** – Fit image to screen

Users who commit to keyboard shortcuts often finish projects in half the time compared to mouse-only users. If your editing tool allows for custom shortcut mapping, consider customizing them based on your workflow.

Chapter 2

Understanding the Interface in 2025

Working efficiently with editing software begins with familiarity. Knowing where tools are placed, how they behave in different modes, and how to shift between environments gives you control over your workflow. The user interface has evolved, but the core principle remains: everything you need should be within reach, visible, and adaptable to your project's demands.

Home Screen Deep Dive

The moment you launch the program, you're presented with the home screen. Though often overlooked, this hub provides entry points to all essential functions and shortcuts for frequent tasks.

Layout Overview

The home screen is structured into clean sections, each guiding you to a particular feature set. Here's a breakdown:

- **Open Projects**: Displays your most recently edited files for quick access.

- **Photo Bin Access**: A button to manage multiple open files during an editing session.

- **Training and How-To Links**: If tutorials are available, they usually populate here.

- **Create and Share**: Offers quick paths to common outputs such as collages, slideshows, or digital greeting cards.

- **Auto Creations or Suggestions**: On some setups, the software auto-generates effects or presentations based on your existing images. This feature can often be disabled if you prefer a more manual approach.

Customizing the Home Experience

You can personalize the home screen by adjusting what appears at startup:

- Decide whether the program opens directly to the editor or organizer

- Hide automated tips or promotional banners

- Adjust startup speed by toggling content preview features

These options are usually found under preferences or settings accessible from the home screen's top bar.

Workspace Modes: Quick, Guided, Expert

Editing is offered through three distinct modes, each designed for a different level of experience or task complexity. Choosing the right mode improves efficiency and keeps the interface uncluttered.

Quick Mode

This mode is built for simplicity. It provides basic controls for color, brightness, contrast, sharpness, and cropping. Sliders dominate this interface, allowing you to see changes in real time.

Ideal For:

- Rapid corrections

- Social media-ready edits

- Batch fixes for color or lighting issues

You won't find advanced layering tools here, but it's the fastest route for casual work.

Guided Mode

Here, you'll find step-by-step workflows that walk you through common or advanced edits. Each guide focuses on a specific task — such as replacing a background or applying a portrait effect — and offers visual cues and on-screen instructions.

Best Suited For:

- Users transitioning from beginner to intermediate

- Tasks with predictable outcomes like photo restorations or color swaps

Each step is clearly explained, and once completed, you can switch to Expert mode for additional refinements.

Expert Mode

This is the full editing environment. All tools become available, including layers, masks, selection brushes, type tools, custom filters, and detailed adjustments.

Built For:

- Professional-level retouching

- Composite image creation

- Creative design projects

In this mode, panels are modular and can be moved, resized, or closed. You're given full control over the layout, and more importantly, over how you want to build your project.

Navigating Panels, Tools, and Contextual Menus

Once inside the editor, the interface is built around a left-to-right and top-to-bottom logic. Understanding the visual structure helps reduce time spent hunting for features.

Toolbar

Located vertically along the left side of the screen, this bar contains all essential tools: selection tools, cropping, brush tools, healing, type, shape, and zoom functions.

Hovering over any tool reveals its name and shortcut key. For tools with variations (like different selection types), right-clicking opens a contextual menu with all options.

Options Bar

Positioned at the top, this area changes based on which tool is selected. If you're using the Brush Tool, this bar will display settings like size, hardness, opacity, and blending options. These controls adjust the behavior of the currently active tool.

Panels

On the right, you'll find multiple panels stacked vertically. These can include:

- **Layers**: Where you view and manage layer hierarchy

- **Effects**: For applying filters and stylistic changes

- **Graphics or Textures**: Preset shapes or elements

- **Adjustments**: Fine-tuning brightness, saturation, and tone

Panels can be collapsed or rearranged depending on your screen size and workflow. A dual-monitor setup allows for even greater flexibility.

Contextual Menus

Right-clicking anywhere in the canvas or on a specific layer opens a context menu. These menus offer shortcuts to actions based on your current tool or selected layer, such as duplicating, applying transformations, or adding layer styles.

Understanding how to navigate and trigger these menus saves considerable time, especially during projects with high layer counts or complex editing stages.

Touch-Enabled Devices and Interface Shortcuts

With the growing use of tablets, hybrid laptops, and touchscreen monitors, the software interface now offers enhanced responsiveness for gesture-based input.

Touch Support Features

Many actions that were traditionally mouse-dependent can now be handled through touch:

- **Pinch to Zoom**

- **Swipe to Pan**

- **Tap-and-Hold for Right-Click Functions**

The interface adapts slightly to accommodate finger-based input, enlarging icons and spacing to prevent accidental taps. You can toggle touch mode in the program's preferences menu.

Stylus Optimization

For artists and editors using drawing tablets or stylus pens, pressure sensitivity is typically supported. Brush size, flow, and opacity can be mapped to pen pressure, creating more natural effects.

Make sure pen drivers are fully updated and configured to allow tilt or pressure control if needed.

Keyboard Shortcuts That Boost Efficiency

Even on a touch device, keyboard shortcuts remain invaluable for speeding up repetitive tasks.

Here are some that provide instant benefits:

Shortcut	Function
Ctrl/Cmd + Alt + Z	Step backward through history
Ctrl/Cmd + Shift + I	Invert selection
Ctrl/Cmd + Shift + E	Merge visible layers into one
Ctrl/Cmd + D	Deselect current selection
Tab	Hide all panels for clean preview

Users can customize some of these through the settings menu or assign alternate keys if working on a compact keyboard.

Chapter 3

File Management & Project Workflow

Efficiency is not just about speed — it's about structure. An editor's workflow must account for how files are named, stored, tracked, edited, and exported. The more deliberate your file management process, the more confidently you can tackle complex projects without worrying about losing work, overwriting previous versions, or exporting with the wrong settings. This chapter walks through essential techniques for handling digital image files, protecting your edits, and producing assets ready for specific end uses.

Smart File Naming, Version Control, and Organization

File chaos is a silent productivity killer. When folders are cluttered with unnamed or confusingly labeled files, creative focus gets replaced by frustration. Building a logical and consistent naming and folder strategy ensures that no version is lost and no effort is wasted.

File Naming Best Practices

Instead of relying on default camera-generated names (like *IMG_0042*), apply descriptive, consistent naming formats. Here's a practical structure:

css

```
[ProjectName]_[Subject]_[YYYY-MM-DD]_[Version].filetype
```

Example:

```
PosterDesign_ClientA_2025-04-04_v03.psd
```

This structure instantly communicates:

- **What** the file is for

- **When** it was last modified

- **Which** version it is

Version Control Without Confusion

While file versioning plugins and cloud-based sync tools can help, a basic manual system is more reliable in standalone editing setups:

- Start with `_v01` for the original

- Increment only when **meaningful changes** are made

- Save **major milestones** under clearly marked folders (e.g., "Approved Versions," "Client Edits," or "Archived Concepts")

Avoid editing the only version of a file. Always work from a duplicated copy when making significant adjustments or client-specific tweaks.

Folder Structure That Supports Workflow

Folders should mimic the flow of your creative process. Here's an example layout:

mathematica

```
Project_Folder/
├── Original_Files/
```

```
├── Working_Files/
├── Exported_Assets/
│      ├── Web/
│      └── Print/
├── Reference_Material/
└── Archive/
```

This kind of hierarchy prevents cross-contamination of file types, helps during backups, and makes it easier for future collaborators to understand your work at a glance.

Working with RAW, JPEG, PSD, PNG, and TIFF

Understanding image formats is key to avoiding compression errors, loss of detail, or unnecessary file bloat. Each format has its strengths and weaknesses depending on how and where it will be used.

RAW

RAW files contain uncompressed, sensor-level image data. They allow you to recover highlights, boost shadows, and apply corrections without degrading image quality.

- **Advantages**: High dynamic range, superior color control, non-destructive editing

- **Considerations**: Large file size, requires conversion before sharing or printing

Always retain the original RAW file even after export. It acts as your digital negative.

JPEG

This format is widely compatible and produces small files thanks to compression. It's ideal for fast sharing or web previews, but repeated saves can degrade image quality.

- **Advantages**: Small size, quick loading, universal support

- **Considerations**: Lossy compression, reduced editability after saving

Use JPEG only for finalized versions, not for ongoing editing.

PSD

This is your editable working file, maintaining all layers, masks, adjustment layers, and effects.

- **Advantages**: Full editability, layer preservation, perfect for reworking designs

- **Considerations**: Larger file size, software-specific (not suitable for web export)

Never flatten your PSD until you're certain your editing process is complete.

PNG

Best used for images requiring transparency or when lossless compression is needed.

- **Advantages**: Supports transparency, no loss in quality

- **Considerations**: Larger than JPEGs, limited to 8-bit or 24-bit color

Often used for web graphics, interface elements, or cutouts with transparent backgrounds.

TIFF

A professional-grade format used for high-quality prints or image archiving.

- **Advantages**: Lossless, high-resolution support, ideal for print

- **Considerations**: Very large file sizes, slower to open or render

For print production, TIFF is often a safer choice than JPEG due to its uncompressed fidelity.

Non-Destructive Editing Principles

One of the most important concepts in professional editing is preserving the original image data. Editing destructively means changes are baked into the image — and can't be undone. Non-destructive methods protect the original content while allowing flexible adjustments.

Techniques That Preserve Image Integrity

Use Adjustment Layers

Instead of applying direct changes to exposure, saturation, or contrast, apply **adjustment layers**. These can be toggled, modified, or removed at any time without touching the base image.

Duplicate the Base Layer

Before using tools like Healing Brush, Clone Stamp, or Filters, duplicate the original layer. This creates a buffer that can be deleted or refined later.

Use Layer Masks Instead of Erasing

When hiding parts of an image or blending two layers, never use the eraser. Use a **mask**, which allows you to control visibility using brush strokes and can be reversed or modified.

Convert to Smart Objects

Convert layers to **smart objects** before applying filters. This allows the filters to be editable later, rather than being permanently applied.

Save Progressive Versions

Save copies of your file at major stages. Use structured naming as described earlier to track which edits were done and when.

Exporting: Web vs Print-Ready Assets

Exporting is not just the final step — it defines how your audience will see your work. Export settings must match the purpose of the file, whether that's for screen display or high-resolution print.

For Web or Screen Display

Files intended for websites, social media, or mobile platforms should prioritize fast loading and color accuracy.

- **Recommended Format**: JPEG or PNG

- **Color Mode**: sRGB

- **Resolution**: 72 to 150 PPI

- **Compression**: Medium to high (balancing size and clarity)

- **Dimensions**: Optimized for platform-specific display (e.g., 1080px wide for Instagram posts)

Use web export features that allow you to preview how compression affects image quality before saving.

For Print

Printed media requires the highest image quality and specific color fidelity.

- **Recommended Format**: TIFF or high-quality JPEG

- **Color Mode**: CMYK (if required by printer), otherwise Adobe RGB

- **Resolution**: 300 PPI or higher

- **Dimensions**: Exact physical size in inches or centimeters

- **Bleed and Crop Marks**: Include if required by print service provider

Always consult with the printing service beforehand to confirm preferred formats and color profiles.

Part II
Core Tools & Fundamental Techniques

Chapter 4

Brushes, Selections, and Layers – The Holy Trinity

Every creative project rests on three indispensable pillars: brushes, selections, and layers. These tools form the foundation of all detailed edits, from simple corrections to advanced digital artwork. When understood properly, they function as precision instruments rather than blunt tools — allowing full control over every pixel, adjustment, and stroke. This chapter explores each of these functions in a methodical and practical manner, stripping away myths and reinforcing fundamentals that professionals depend on daily.

Understanding Layer Logic

Layers are not just stacking elements — they define structure, organization, and visual hierarchy. Learning how different layer types behave and interact is key to editing responsibly and flexibly.

Pixel Layers

Also known as raster layers, these are the standard layers most users interact with. Any brush stroke, fill, or imported image typically lands on a pixel layer.

- **Editable Content**: Brush marks, retouching, imported photos

- **Limitation**: Destructive when changes are made directly

- **Recommendation**: Always duplicate original images before editing directly on a pixel layer

Adjustment Layers

These are non-destructive modifiers that apply visual effects (brightness, saturation, contrast, etc.) across one or multiple layers beneath them. They do **not** contain image data.

- **Benefit**: Fully reversible, can be masked or reconfigured anytime

- **Common Types**: Hue/Saturation, Levels, Curves, Black & White

- **Use Case**: Color grading or exposure correction without harming the original layer

Text Layers

Text layers are vector-based and remain editable until rasterized. They are crucial for projects that involve typography, captions, or design elements that require clean scaling.

- **Editable**: Font, size, tracking, alignment

- **Non-Destructive**: Can be modified without quality loss

- **Reminder**: Keep text layers live for future revisions, only rasterize when necessary for special effects

Smart Layers

Also referred to as embedded objects, these layers allow filters and transformations without affecting the original data.

- **Key Advantage**: Filters applied to smart layers remain editable

- **Example**: A photo filter like Gaussian blur can be toggled or changed without reapplying

- **Workflow Tip**: Convert important assets to smart layers before applying advanced transformations

---

Selections: Lasso, Quick, Object, and Refine Edge Techniques

Selections define where edits occur. Whether you're cutting out a subject, isolating a color range, or making precise adjustments, clean selections ensure clean results.

Lasso Tools: Precision and Freeform Control

Freehand Lasso

Ideal for quick selections with rough shapes, this tool relies entirely on manual control.

- **Advantage**: Fast for broad areas or initial masks

- **Drawback**: Less accurate, best used with a graphics tablet or mouse with good control

Polygonal Lasso

Works best for selecting objects with straight lines or angular shapes.

- **Tip**: Combine with zoom for pixel-perfect selections around edges like buildings or borders

Magnetic Lasso

Automatically snaps to high-contrast edges, which speeds up selections on clearly defined subjects.

- **Use Case**: Ideal for tracing around people, objects, or text when contrast is strong

- **Caution**: May struggle with low-contrast areas or textured backgrounds

Quick Selection Tool: Speed Meets Intelligence

This tool uses brush-like strokes to grow the selection area based on texture and contrast. It's ideal for fast selections of complex shapes.

- **Usage Tip**: Start broad, then subtract unwanted areas by holding a modifier key

- **Strength**: Real-time adjustments, excellent for general cut-outs or grouping tones

Object Selection: Modern Automation

Modern software updates have introduced AI-assisted object detection. This feature attempts to isolate people, products, or dominant elements automatically.

- **Use Case**: Fast subject isolation for headshots, product images, or social media graphics

- **Limitation**: Results may vary based on image complexity — always double-check edges

Refine Edge and Masking Techniques

After a selection is made, perfecting its boundaries is critical. This is where the refine edge tool comes in — especially useful for soft elements like hair, fur, or transparent fabrics.

- **Options Available**: Smooth, feather, contrast, and shift edge

- **Refine Hair Button** (if available in your software): Traces hairline and fills in gaps without manual masking

- **Best Practice**: Zoom in to 200% and work around the selection edge gradually using feather and contrast for realism

---

Brush Mastery: Custom Brushes, Opacity Flow, and Blending Modes

Brush tools offer infinite control over how changes are applied — from subtle shading to dramatic texturing. But mastering brushes means more than knowing where they are. You must know how they behave.

Creating and Managing Custom Brushes

Custom brushes let you define how texture, shape, spacing, and rotation behave in each stroke.

- **Creating a Brush**:

  o Start with a black-and-white shape on a blank canvas

  o Use the "Define Brush Preset" or equivalent function

  o Save and label it clearly under a custom brush folder

- **Brush Tips**:

  - Keep shapes simple for versatility

  - Use hard edges for stamps, soft edges for painting

  - Consider spacing and scatter settings for texture effects

Opacity and Flow: The Difference Explained

Many confuse these two settings, but they serve different purposes.

- **Opacity** controls the **maximum transparency** of each stroke — even if you go over the same area repeatedly, it won't build up past the set level

- **Flow** controls the **rate of buildup** — going over an area multiple times darkens it gradually

Use Case:

- For shading or retouching skin, a low flow gives smooth transitions

- For sharp edits or strong coloring, raise opacity but lower flow

Blending Modes: How Layers Interact

Blending modes control how brush strokes and layers interact with what's underneath them. They are often misunderstood but are incredibly useful when used properly.

- **Multiply**: Darkens anything it touches. Excellent for shadows.

- **Screen**: Lightens content, useful for glows or highlights.

- **Overlay**: Enhances contrast and vibrance.

- **Soft Light**: Adds gentle emphasis without overpowering the base.

- **Color**: Changes hue/saturation without affecting brightness

Tip: Always apply blending modes to a duplicated layer or an empty layer filled with neutral gray to maintain flexibility.

Chapter 5

The Power of Adjustment Layers and Filters

Editing is not just about what you add, but how precisely you control and refine what's already there. In a professional workflow, adjustment layers and filters operate as surgical tools—quietly shaping light, tone, and form beneath the surface. This chapter provides a precise breakdown of these tools, guiding you through practical usage, not just what they are but how they're best used with accuracy.

Using Brightness/Contrast, Levels, and Curves Like a Technician

Brightness/Contrast: The Blunt Yet Useful Tool

This adjustment is the most straightforward, but its simplicity can be both a strength and a limitation.

- **Brightness** raises or lowers overall lightness uniformly across all tones

- **Contrast** increases the separation between light and dark areas

When to Use:

- Quick corrections on well-exposed images

- Fixing slightly dull or faded visuals

- Avoid on photos where highlights or shadows need selective adjustments

Caution: Raising contrast too high can cause loss of detail in bright or dark regions.

Levels: Targeted Control Over Tonal Range

Levels give you direct control over black, midtone, and white points.

- **Histogram Display** shows the current tonal distribution

- **Input Sliders** adjust where shadows start, midtones shift, and highlights end

- **Output Sliders** compress the range for more subtle grading

How to Use Like a Technician:

- Pull the black slider inward until it touches the start of the histogram data

- Do the same from the right with the white slider

- Move the midtone (gray) slider to adjust overall brightness without clipping

Curves: The Advanced Technician's Playground

Curves offer complete freedom in manipulating tonal values across the brightness spectrum.

- **Anchor Points** can be placed along the curve to isolate shadows, midtones, or highlights

- **S-curve** increases contrast by steepening the midtones and expanding shadows and highlights

- **Inverted S-curve** lowers contrast for a flatter, muted look

Use Case:

- Correct color casts by isolating Red, Green, or Blue channels

- Apply local contrast where Levels cannot reach

- Match tone across a batch of product photos or portraits

Color Correction Fundamentals

Color correction isn't about applying filters—it's about returning a photo or composition to a balanced state, where white looks neutral and skin tones appear natural.

Neutralizing Color Casts

Most images taken under mixed lighting tend to lean toward a particular color hue. Identifying and removing that bias is the first step toward correction.

Steps to Neutralize:

1. Use a **Threshold Adjustment Layer** to find true black and white points

2. Apply a **Curves Adjustment**, open the individual RGB channels

3. Balance the color sliders until the image appears neutral

Tip: A properly neutral image will show whites as clean and grays as gray, without any hue shift.

Skin Tone Correction

In portraits, skin is your calibration anchor. Overcorrection leads to orange or green hues that immediately look artificial.

- Use the **Selective Color Adjustment Layer** to subtly target red and yellow channels

- Shift magenta and cyan sliders slightly while monitoring the result

- Always reference real skin photos rather than trusting your monitor's color

Saturation and Vibrance

- **Saturation** boosts all colors equally, which can oversaturate already vivid tones

- **Vibrance** enhances only muted colors while protecting skin tones

Professional Strategy: Apply vibrance first, then use saturation with restraint—if at all.

Filter Gallery vs Smart Filters – What Works Where?

Filter Gallery: Experimental and Aesthetic Modifiers

The filter gallery contains a suite of artistic and visual stylizing options—from glowing edges to texture-enhancing filters.

Best Used For:

- Creative effects for posters, collages, and stylized projects

- Background treatments in digital art

- Simulated textures or lighting effects

Limitation: Filters applied through this gallery are destructive unless used on a duplicate layer or with a smart object.

Smart Filters: Reversible and Non-Destructive

Smart filters are essentially filters applied to layers that have been converted into smart objects. This allows:

- Real-time preview and adjustment

- Masking the filter effect

- Stacking multiple filters with editable parameters

Use Case:

- Applying blur to backgrounds while retaining the ability to update later

- Layering sharpen and noise reduction without damaging original content

- Testing multiple visual outcomes on a single image layer

Workflow Tip: Convert any working layer to a smart object before applying a complex filter. This protects both data and editability.

Dodging, Burning, and Sharpening Without Overdoing It

These are powerful techniques when used with restraint. They enhance texture, direct attention, and define depth—but they can also destroy subtlety if misused.

Dodging: Lightening Specific Areas

Used to bring attention to features or lift shadows in controlled areas.

Best Practice:

- Work on a 50% gray overlay layer set to **Soft Light** blending mode

- Use a soft brush at 5–10% flow for gradual buildup

- Target areas like the eyes, cheekbones, or light spots in still-life compositions

Burning: Darkening Areas for Depth

Used to shape shadows and de-emphasize distracting highlights.

Technique:

- Same 50% gray method applies here

- Focus on under the chin, hairlines, or background edges

- Avoid hard-edged brushes to prevent unrealistic patches

Tip: Zoom out often. Dodging and burning at high zoom can mislead your perception of global tone balance.

Sharpening: Enhancing Texture, Not Noise

Sharpening should highlight detail without creating artifacts.

- **High Pass Filter**:

- ○ Duplicate the layer

- ○ Apply **High Pass** at a radius of 1–2 pixels

- ○ Set the blend mode to **Overlay** or **Soft Light**

- **Unsharp Mask**:

  - ○ Use with restraint: Threshold 2–4, Amount below 100%

  - ○ Always compare before/after at 100% zoom

Sharpen Last: Always perform sharpening after resizing or cropping your final output. Sharpening too early locks you into a visual sharpness level that may not translate well across print and screen.

Chapter 6

Retouching and Restoration

Image editing is not always about creativity—it often requires technical skill, precision, and subtlety. Restoration and retouching demand patience and a sharp eye. Whether you're repairing family photographs that have survived the years or refining high-resolution portraits for clients, understanding how to manipulate pixels without leaving fingerprints is what separates good work from outstanding craftsmanship.

Clone Stamp vs Healing Brush vs Content-Aware

Clone Stamp: Full Manual Control

The Clone Stamp tool is a direct copy-and-paste approach. You sample from one part of an image and paint that sample elsewhere.

Best Used For:

- Repeating patterns such as bricks, textiles, or wood grain

- Filling in hard-edged objects or clean geometry

- Areas where texture must match precisely

Technique Tips:

- Always sample from a clean and similar tone area

- Use a soft brush edge to blend borders smoothly

- Sample frequently to avoid visible repetition

When It Fails: The Clone Stamp does not blend or correct lighting. You are responsible for all visual alignment.

Healing Brush: Texture + Tone Integration

Unlike the Clone Stamp, the Healing Brush blends the sampled texture with the surrounding tone and color of the destination area.

Best Used For:

- Minor blemishes or inconsistencies in skin or fabric

- Small scratches or stains

- Seamless blending of low-contrast elements

Technique Tips:

- Keep brush size slightly larger than the imperfection

- Sample from areas close in lighting and color

- Use a low flow setting for layered, gradual corrections

Content-Aware Fill: Letting the Software Predict

Content-Aware Fill analyzes the surrounding image and auto-fills the selected region based on context.

Best Used For:

- Removing isolated subjects from backgrounds

- Clearing wires from skies, street signs, or patches of pavement

- Filling gaps in panoramas

Limitations:

- Not reliable near high-contrast edges or overlapping elements

- May produce noise or repeating textures if overused

Best Practice: After applying, inspect the filled area at 100% zoom. If the result is inconsistent, clean it manually with the Healing Brush or Clone Stamp.

Fixing Old Photos: Dust, Tears, and Fading

Photographs, especially printed ones, carry physical evidence of time. Whether it's creases from mishandling or yellowing from years in storage, digital restoration allows you to restore what was lost without compromising the original's integrity.

Removing Dust and Scratches

Dust often appears as white specks or hairline marks. The first step is scanning the photo at high resolution.

Method:

- Use the **Spot Healing Brush** on each visible dust particle

- For large areas, use **Filter > Noise > Dust & Scratches** at low thresholds

- Set a layer to **Darken** mode and paint gently with sampled color to patch subtle areas

Repairing Tears and Creases

Creases require texture rebuilding and tone matching.

Step-by-Step:

1. Zoom into the crease

2. Use the **Clone Stamp** to fill consistent textures like fabric, sky, or background

3. Blend edges with the **Healing Brush**

4. Use **Dodge and Burn** on a neutral gray layer to even out residual lighting imbalance

Addressing Fading and Discoloration

Faded photos often lean toward yellow, blue, or magenta due to chemical breakdown.

Correction Workflow:

- Apply **Curves** or **Levels** to restore contrast

- Use **Color Balance** to shift dominant hues back to neutral

- Adjust **Hue/Saturation** to control specific color channels

For black-and-white photos, restore contrast and eliminate discoloration by converting to grayscale and rebalancing highlights and shadows.

Smoothing Skin Without Losing Texture

Soft skin is desirable, but completely erasing texture leads to unnatural results. The goal is to retain natural skin detail while minimizing blemishes, discoloration, and harsh lighting.

Frequency Separation: Texture vs Tone

This method separates an image into two layers—one for fine detail (texture), another for color and tone (low frequency).

Basic Setup:

1. Duplicate image twice

2. Apply Gaussian Blur to the lower layer (around 4–10px radius)

3. Apply **Apply Image** (subtract or add) on the upper layer to isolate texture

4. Edit color/tone on the blurred layer and clean fine detail on the texture layer

Tools for Tone Layer:

- Healing Brush

- Patch Tool

- Soft-edged brush with low opacity

Tools for Texture Layer:

- Clone Stamp at 100% flow

- Light dodging or burning

This process keeps pores, fine lines, and skin realism while cleaning up color blotches and uneven tones.

Simpler Method: Low-Flow Healing + Blur

If you're not using frequency separation:

1. Use **Healing Brush** at 10–15% flow to clean blemishes

2. Add a **Duplicate Layer**, apply **Surface Blur** with threshold control

3. Mask the blur and paint only over rough areas

4. Avoid using blur on detailed zones like eyes, lips, and hair

---

Removing Objects Cleanly (People, Wires, Blemishes)

When removing elements from images, the challenge is not deleting them—it's making it look like they were never there.

Removing People from Backgrounds

- **Select the Subject** using Lasso or Object Selection

- Apply **Content-Aware Fill** on the selected area

- Inspect for artifacts, and repair leftover edges with Clone Stamp or Healing Brush

- For complex patterns, duplicate surrounding textures manually and blend

Tip: If the background is simple (like sand or sky), use large feathered selections. If complex (like crowds or fences), work in smaller segments.

Removing Wires and Lines

Wires cutting across skies or walls can be distracting.

Method:

- Use **Spot Healing Brush** in a single stroke

- If alignment fails, switch to **Clone Stamp** and sample sky gradient nearby

- Clean sharp areas (edges of buildings or poles) with a fine-tipped Healing Brush

Bonus Tip: To straighten a cloned line or texture, hold Shift while using the Clone Stamp between two points.

Removing Blemishes or Minor Distractions

Small skin imperfections, light reflections, or sensor dust can be fixed with speed.

- Use **Spot Healing** or **Healing Brush**

- Work on a separate layer to maintain flexibility

- Toggle visibility on/off often to maintain perspective

Part III
Creative Editing & Artistic Techniques

Chapter 7

Compositing Magic – From Cutouts to Concept Art

Compositing is not a trick—it's a discipline. Whether it's replacing a dull sky with a vivid one, creating a cinematic poster from several photos, or constructing surreal concept art, the craft of combining visual elements must be handled with precision and consistency. The real challenge isn't just cutting things out and pasting them elsewhere—it's making those pieces look like they've always belonged together.

A well-executed composite can make viewers forget that it was ever built from separate images. That level of quality requires close attention to details: light direction, color temperature, shadows, scale, and perspective. This chapter will guide you through each step of making believable and beautiful composite work, from background swaps to intricate, multi-layered scenes.

Background Replacements Done Right

Replacing a background is one of the most common compositing tasks. But doing it right requires more than cutting and pasting. It's about accurate selection, clean masking, and tone blending that maintains the subject's realism within the new scene.

Step 1: Precise Subject Extraction

The foundation of a successful replacement starts with an accurate cutout.

Techniques for clean cutouts:

- Use **Select Subject** followed by **Select and Mask** for automatic but editable results

- For subjects with hair, enable **Refine Hair** and use the **Refine Edge Brush** around soft edges

- On solid backgrounds, manual **Pen Tool** selections offer precision for crisp edges

- Feather the edge slightly to avoid unnatural sharpness

Tip: Always extract on a separate layer. Keep a copy of the original in case refinement is needed later.

Step 2: Choose a Matching Background

The background must support the story and fit with the subject. Consider the **light direction**, **horizon line**, and **focus depth** of the subject before choosing.

Checklist:

- Is the light coming from the same direction?

- Does the perspective match? (e.g., eye level, looking up or down)

- Is the color temperature similar? Warm sunset vs cool shade?

- Does the resolution and noise level of the background match the subject?

If not, it will look forced—no matter how good the cutout is.

Step 3: Blending with Adjustments

After placing the subject over the new background:

- Apply **Curves** or **Levels** to match brightness

- Use **Color Balance** or **Selective Color** to match overall tint

- Consider **Gaussian Blur** on the background to simulate realistic depth of field

- Add subtle shadows under feet or objects to anchor the subject in place

Soft shadows can be created with an **elliptical black gradient on a new layer** set to Multiply or Overlay, blurred for realism.

Matching Light, Color, and Perspective

Even when the elements are technically correct, compositing falls apart when lighting, color, and camera angles don't align. These three elements must be in sync for the viewer to believe the image is real.

Matching Light Direction and Quality

Look at your subject and background. Where is the light source coming from? Is it hard or soft? Diffused or directional?

Correction Tips:

- Use **Curves Adjustment Layers** to simulate stronger light on one side of the subject

- Apply a **Gradient Map** set to Soft Light for overall lighting harmony

- Use **Dodge and Burn** layers (on 50% gray in Overlay mode) to strengthen or soften shadows manually

If necessary, create **fake shadows** behind objects using soft brushes with lower opacity and Gaussian blur.

Matching Color Temperature

Subjects shot under different lighting will often carry unwanted color casts. You'll need to neutralize those before adjusting to match the background.

Steps:

1. Neutralize color casts with **Camera Raw Filter** or **Color Balance**

2. Match the overall tone using **Curves** or **Hue/Saturation**

3. Use **Photo Filter** to gently warm or cool an image globally

For finer control, use **Selective Color** to target specific tones (like shadows or midtones).

Matching Perspective

Even small mismatches in camera angle or scale can make a composite look unnatural.

Quick Checks:

- Match horizon lines between foreground and background

- Align vanishing points if architectural elements are involved

- Resize subjects so they appear consistent with the focal length and angle of the background

Use **Transform > Perspective** to nudge layers into visual agreement. Don't overdo this, as it can distort natural shapes.

Layer Masks vs Clipping Masks

Understanding the difference between layer masks and clipping masks will save you hours of confusion during compositing work.

Layer Masks: Non-Destructive Visibility Control

A **layer mask** hides or reveals portions of the attached layer based on black (hide), white (show), and gray (partial) areas.

Use Cases:

- Blending parts of one image into another

- Soft fading transitions

- Removing edges without erasing pixels

Best Practice: Always use a layer mask instead of erasing. It lets you change your mind later.

Clipping Masks: Targeted Adjustments

A **clipping mask** allows one layer to only affect the visibility of the layer beneath it.

Use Cases:

- Applying a texture or adjustment to only one image or object

- Adding lighting or color correction to a specific cutout

- Painting highlights or shadows on a subject without spilling onto the background

How to Create:

- Place your adjustment or paint layer above the target

- Right-click and choose "Create Clipping Mask" or hold `Alt` (Windows) / `Option` (Mac) and click between the two layers

These masks can be stacked. You can have a masked layer that also acts as a clipping mask for another adjustment.

Creating Seamless Multi-Image Blends

Bringing multiple photos into one scene is the essence of complex compositing. Whether you're building a sci-fi background from several locations or layering animals into surreal portraits, the key to realism lies in controlled chaos—organizing elements while disguising seams.

Step-by-Step Guide to Seamless Blending

1. **Sketch a Layout First**
   Think like a set designer. Block out where each major visual element will sit before importing images. This keeps composition balanced.

2. **Import and Organize Elements**
   Bring in your source images, placing each on its own layer or folder. Label them clearly for fast access.

3. **Cut and Mask Cleanly**
   Use advanced selections and edge refining techniques discussed earlier. If objects are semi-transparent, such as smoke or veils, use soft masks and build layers gradually.

4. **Use Adjustment Layers to Match Tone**

   Each image likely comes from a different source. Apply matching curves, levels, and hue shifts on a per-image basis until they start feeling cohesive.

5. **Add Atmospheric Unity**

   This could mean adding fog, colored light, or texture overlays. A subtle noise layer or light mist overlay helps tie different elements together.

6. **Control Depth Using Blur and Lighting**

   Use **Gaussian Blur** to push distant objects back. Paint highlights and shadows using Overlay layers to simulate direction and depth.

7. **Finish with Global Adjustments**

   Add an overall **Color Lookup**, **Gradient Map**, or **Curves Layer** above the entire composition. This creates harmony across all visual pieces.

Chapter 8

Typography, Design, and Graphic Layouts

Typography is more than picking a font. It's about clarity, tone, and visual rhythm. Design without structured type is like a song with off-beat instruments—disorganized, noisy, and easily forgotten. This chapter focuses on mastering text tools, understanding how to apply visual effects that enhance (rather than overwhelm), and learning to create functional, polished layouts for social media and print materials alike.

Whether you're crafting a flyer, designing a web banner, or building promotional graphics, your use of typography and layout will either elevate the message or dilute it. Let's explore how to structure design elements with purpose and polish.

Working with Text Tools and Type Layers

Photoshop (and similar software) provides powerful control over type, but many users limit themselves to typing out a sentence and picking a font. There's far more to harness when you understand type layers as editable, flexible design components.

Creating and Editing Type Layers

- Use the **Horizontal Type Tool** (T key) for standard text entries

- For vertical arrangements, switch to the **Vertical Type Tool**

- Once placed, text remains editable until rasterized—avoid flattening unless necessary

- Type layers can hold paragraph formatting, alignment, spacing, and more

Editable Features Include:

- Font family and style (bold, italic, etc.)

- Size and leading (line spacing)

- Kerning (space between characters)

- Tracking (space across a word or block)

- Paragraph justification and indentation

All of this is available in the **Character** and **Paragraph** panels, which should be kept visible during any text-heavy work.

Converting Text to Shapes or Paths

For design purposes (like logos or custom artwork), you may want to **convert type to a shape**.

How to do it:

- Right-click the type layer → **Convert to Shape**

- This transforms letters into vector outlines, editable with the **Path Selection Tool** or **Direct Selection Tool**

- Note: This makes the text non-editable as text. Keep a backup layer in case you need to change the wording.

Use this when you need to warp individual characters, apply custom fills, or integrate type tightly into illustrations.

Text Effects: Glow, Warp, and Stroke

While text should always be legible, it doesn't have to be plain. Simple effects—when used with restraint—can add depth and visual energy.

Outer Glow and Drop Shadow

Used to separate text from complex backgrounds or add ambient light.

- **Outer Glow**: Found in the **Layer Styles** menu

    ○ Choose a color, adjust spread and size

    ○ Use soft tones for subtle lighting effects

- **Drop Shadow**: Also within Layer Styles

    ○ Adjust angle to match existing lighting

    ○ Use distance and spread to control shadow behavior

    ○ Avoid harsh shadows unless it's for stylized poster work

Note: These effects should enhance readability—not distract from it.

Stroke (Outline)

- Found under **Layer Style > Stroke**

- Choose position: Outside (cleanest), Inside, or Center

- Keep stroke width proportional to font size

- Use for clarity over busy backgrounds or to emphasize short words

Avoid neon or saturated outlines unless the style specifically demands it. For print, always test visibility on white and dark backgrounds.

Warping Text

- Use **Edit > Transform > Warp** for manual warping

- Or apply **Type Warp** from the top bar when a type layer is active

- Common warp styles include Arc, Bulge, Wave, and Flag

This is useful for stylized titles, emblems, or retro signage effects. Be careful—over-warped text can become unreadable. Apply with a light hand.

Creating Social Media Banners, Flyers, and Mockups

Designs meant for digital sharing need different handling than print. Screen resolution, layout size, and message hierarchy must be optimized for quick consumption.

Social Media Banners

Platform-Specific Sizes (2025 Standards):

- Instagram Post: 1080 x 1080 px

- Facebook Cover: 1640 x 624 px

- YouTube Channel Art: 2560 x 1440 px (safe zone: 1546 x 423 px)

- Twitter/X Header: 1500 x 500 px

Best Practices:

- Keep text in center "safe zones"

- Use bold typefaces for legibility

- Contrast is crucial—avoid light gray on white

- Optimize image resolution to 72–100 PPI for screens

Flyer and Poster Design

Flyers require a stronger focus on visual flow.

Key Structure:

1. **Headline** – Bold and large, grabs attention

2. **Subhead** – Supports headline with clarity

3. **Body Text** – Clear, not cluttered; use bullet points or icons

4. **Call to Action** – What should the viewer do next? Visit? Buy? Attend?

Tip: Keep fonts to 2 or 3 per design. Overloading with font styles weakens credibility.

Mockup Creation

Use smart objects to present your work professionally.

Steps to Build a Mockup:

- Start with a high-res photo (e.g., paper, phone screen, billboard)

- Create a placeholder layer and convert it to a **Smart Object**

- Double-click the Smart Object to place your design

- Save and return to the mockup—your design appears in realistic perspective

Mockups are ideal for clients, portfolios, and product previews.

Layout Best Practices for Web & Print

Design layout isn't just about where things go—it's about creating visual paths that guide the viewer naturally through the information.

Web Layouts

Grid Systems:

- Use 12-column grids for flexible, responsive layouts

- Define clear padding and margin spacing

- Use typographic hierarchy—titles, subheads, and body sizes should be noticeably distinct

Color and Fonts:

- Stick to web-safe fonts or Google Fonts for compatibility

- Use hex values for exact color control

- Aim for color contrast ratios of 4.5:1 or higher for accessibility

Interactive Design Tips:

- Buttons should stand out, be easy to click

- Link text should be clearly distinguished from body copy

- Use hover effects sparingly and consistently

Print Layouts

DPI and Dimensions:

- Standard print resolution: **300 DPI**

- CMYK color mode required (not RGB)

- Leave **bleed space** (typically 0.125 inch) beyond the edges for trimming

Margins and Balance:

- Use wider margins than screen designs

- Align text and visuals to an invisible baseline or column grid

- Avoid crowding the edges—white space is not wasted space

Text Considerations:

- Serif fonts are easier to read in long print blocks

- Avoid font sizes under 8pt

- Always proof print to check readability and color consistency

Chapter 9

Guided Edits That Don't Look Cheesy

Editing software often provides shortcuts for those without technical expertise—but shortcuts don't have to look cheap. When used thoughtfully, even the most basic guided tools can lead to impressive results that appear handcrafted. This chapter focuses on using built-in features without sacrificing originality. It also explores stylized edits such as double exposures, pop art renditions, and subtle depth-of-field tricks. Additionally, we will unpack modern hybrid visuals like cinemagraphs and attention-grabbing collages—tools that can elevate social content and marketing visuals alike.

Making the Most of Built-In Tools

Photoshop Elements and similar software offer **guided editing panels** that simplify complex processes into step-by-step workflows. These tools are typically seen as entry-level, but with refined choices and good taste, they can produce results equal to advanced techniques.

Understanding Guided Edits

Guided Edits are categorized into themes such as:

- **Basic adjustments** (brightness, contrast, sharpening)

- **Color enhancements** (tinting, duotone effects)

- **Photographic effects** (vignettes, high key, low key)

- **Fun edits** (motion blur, puzzle effect, reflections)

- **Special edits** (double exposure, background replacement)

While many of these options are designed for casual users, combining them selectively allows for professional-grade output.

How to Keep Guided Edits Looking Tasteful

Here's what separates cheesy from clever:

- **Less is more**: Don't apply every feature in one go. Limit effects to one or two enhancements per image.

- **Adjust default sliders**: Don't rely on presets. After applying a guided effect, use the manual sliders to reduce intensity.

- **Blend edits manually**: After running a guided process, switch to **Expert Mode**. Refine the layers using masks, blend modes, or opacity settings.

- **Use non-destructive editing**: Always duplicate your layer before applying a guided edit. This protects your original and gives you flexibility to reverse changes.

- **Focus on purpose**: Every edit should support the message of the image. If an effect adds nothing meaningful, skip it.

By treating built-in tools as a starting point rather than a final product, you gain control while speeding up your workflow.

Stylized Effects: Double Exposure, Pop Art, and Depth-of-Field Illusions

Stylized effects are often associated with overdone filters, but they don't have to be. When executed with care, they can create compelling visuals that attract attention without looking gimmicky.

Double Exposure

This technique overlays two images to create a surreal, layered visual.

How to do it tastefully:

1. Choose a portrait with clear contrast (head-and-shoulders works best)

2. Select a textured background (cityscape, forest, abstract pattern)

3. Use the **Blend Mode: Screen or Lighten** for the top image

4. Add a mask and use a soft brush to blend edges manually

5. Adjust the opacity to ensure the face remains recognizable

Key to success: Allow one image to lead visually. Both shouldn't fight for attention.

Pop Art Treatment

This graphic style mimics retro screen printing and works best on portraits and objects.

Steps to achieve a clean pop art look:

1. Convert photo to black-and-white using **Threshold** adjustment

2. Use the **Posterize** function to reduce colors to 4–6 tones

3. Fill each area with bold, flat colors using **Solid Color Adjustment Layers**

4. Add thick outlines with the **Find Edges** filter or by duplicating and stroking the selection

To keep the aesthetic polished:

- Avoid blurring effects

- Stick with a controlled palette (no more than 5 vibrant colors)

- Use halftone brushes for texture, not default pixel noise

Depth-of-Field Simulations

Shallow depth-of-field draws focus to one subject while blurring the background.

To simulate this digitally:

1. Duplicate the image layer

2. On the background copy, apply **Gaussian Blur** (radius depends on resolution, but typically 8–15px)

3. Add a layer mask and use a black brush to reveal the subject from the sharp original

4. Feather the mask edges to create natural transitions

You can also apply **Lens Blur** with a depth map for more realistic separation if your software allows.

Avoid over-blurring—it should suggest lens behavior, not feel like a smear filter.

Cinemagraphs, Collages, and Scroll-Stopping Visuals

Modern editing isn't confined to static pictures. Hybrid visuals—where motion and stillness intersect—are becoming increasingly common on social platforms and digital ads.

Cinemagraphs: Controlled Motion in Still Frames

A cinemagraph is a looped video where only a portion of the frame moves. The rest remains frozen, creating a hypnotic visual.

How to make one:

1. Record a tripod-stabilized video (3–5 seconds long)

2. Import into software that supports timeline editing

3. Duplicate the video layer

4. Convert the top layer to a still frame (rasterize or select a still frame as a freeze)

5. Add a mask and use a soft brush to reveal movement only in a targeted area (e.g., pouring water, waving cloth)

6. Loop the footage and export as a GIF or MP4

Keep motion subtle. The point isn't to animate the whole scene—it's to surprise the viewer with an isolated flicker of life.

Collage Work Without Chaos

Collages can easily become messy when images compete. The solution lies in planning composition before you start dropping in content.

Rules for a refined collage:

- **Choose a unifying color theme**

- **Stick to consistent lighting or adjust image tones to match**

- **Use clean, white borders or consistent shadowing for image separation**

- **Avoid unnecessary overlays and stickers** unless you're doing themed promos

Create balance through asymmetry. Don't line up everything symmetrically—let the visual weight distribute naturally.

Scroll-Stopping Visuals

These are images that catch attention immediately when someone is skimming online content. The secret isn't noise—it's clarity.

Design strategies that hold attention:

- Use contrast: Black and white with a splash of one vivid color

- Create tension: Unusual crops, off-center subjects, or extreme angles

- Add minimal motion: Subtle flickers, blinking eyes, moving lights

- Incorporate bold typography layered over visuals with careful legibility

Avoid:

- Generic lens flares

- Grunge filters over sharp portraits

- Stock overlays (unless customized or created from scratch)

Chapter 10

Creative Projects to Build Your Portfolio

One of the most effective ways to grow as a digital designer is to consistently create and compile projects that showcase technical ability, creativity, and visual problem-solving. A well-curated portfolio tells a story about your growth, your personal style, and your adaptability to various design needs. This chapter outlines four practical yet creative projects that not only sharpen your editing skills but also serve as polished additions to a client-ready portfolio.

Each project has been selected to represent a different type of design scenario—documentary-style storytelling, high-end retouching, digital merchandising, and visual concept development. The emphasis is not on flair for the sake of flair, but on how thoughtfully constructed images reflect professionalism and control.

Photo Diary Layouts

Photo diaries, also known as visual journals or narrative grids, are a blend of documentary photography and layout storytelling. Unlike random photo dumps, these layouts are purposeful—they guide the viewer's eye through a specific day, trip, or theme.

Purpose

This project demonstrates:

- Narrative design skills

- Cohesion in visual style

- Layout balancing with images and text

- Image sequence logic (event flow)

How to Build a Photo Diary Layout

Step 1: Select a story-worthy event or theme
Choose a simple story: a morning routine, weekend hike, or visit to a street market. It doesn't need to be exotic; it just needs clear visuals and emotion.

Step 2: Curate 8–12 photos with consistency
Avoid including every image from your camera roll. Choose shots that contrast wide angles with close details, and ensure they share similar lighting and tone.

Step 3: Create a structured grid
Use a **modular grid**—a 2x2, 3x3, or asymmetric layout with white space padding. Maintain consistent spacing between frames.

Step 4: Add subtle captions
Don't crowd the page with paragraphs. A few lines under key images or at the corners can guide context.

Step 5: Use neutral or off-white backgrounds
Let the photos take center stage. Avoid texture backgrounds unless they serve a thematic purpose.

Step 6: Export at high resolution
Photo diaries should print cleanly or be viewed crisply on high-resolution devices.

Tips for Refinement

- Desaturate slightly for a timeless look

- Overlay soft film grain for texture

- Use grid alignment tools for precision

- Don't center every image—create natural motion across the page

Photo diaries show your ability to document moments with design awareness—not just photography.

Magazine-Style Portrait Retouches

Editorial retouching is not about blurring skin into plastic—it's about enhancing texture, color balance, and light so that the portrait remains lifelike, but elevated. This type of work shows technical control and restraint, key qualities in professional image editing.

Purpose

This project demonstrates:

- High-end retouching workflow

- Attention to skin tone and detail

- Layer-based editing control

- Understanding of light direction and shadow retention

Building the Project

Step 1: Choose a high-resolution portrait
Work with RAW files or uncompressed JPEGs. Ensure sharpness, natural lighting, and a clean background.

Step 2: Frequency separation for skin
Split the texture and color tones onto separate layers. Use the **High Pass filter** for texture and **Gaussian Blur** for tonal base.

Step 3: Dodge and burn on a 50% gray layer
Use soft white and black brushes (set to low opacity) to paint subtle highlights and shadows. This technique sculpts the face and preserves dimensionality.

Step 4: Correct color cast
Add a **Color Balance** or **Selective Color** adjustment layer. Target shadows and midtones to neutralize tints without destroying skin hue.

Step 5: Sharpening and eye clarity
Zoom in and selectively sharpen the iris, lips, and brows. Avoid over-sharpening skin.

Step 6: Apply background separation
Duplicate the subject layer, mask out the person, and blur the background slightly to create optical separation.

Final Layout

Present your final portrait on a white or soft grey canvas with a vertical magazine frame. Add a mock headline, date, and nameplate to give it a polished editorial look.

Product Mockups for Digital Shops and Print-on-Demand

If you're offering goods online—whether stickers, t-shirts, mugs, or planners—mockups are essential. They help buyers visualize your design in context. Good mockups look real, not flat. Your portfolio should show your ability to integrate your artwork seamlessly into product photography.

Purpose

This project demonstrates:

- Smart object and layer masking proficiency

- Color adjustment skills

- Realistic texture overlays and lighting

How to Create Product Mockups

Step 1: Source a blank product photo
 Use a royalty-free image or photograph your own blank item on a clean surface with soft lighting.

Step 2: Design your graphic separately
 Keep your artwork vector-based (SVG or PNG) with a transparent background. This preserves sharpness when scaled.

Step 3: Convert the product layer into a smart object
 This allows for non-destructive placement and later edits.

Step 4: Match lighting and shadows
 Use Multiply or Overlay blending modes to apply the design over product contours. Manually paint in subtle shadows or highlights to match folds or edges.

Step 5: Add a reflective layer or paper texture
 This gives your design the appearance of being printed or pressed on the product, not floating above it.

Step 6: Export multiple variations
 Show the product in different colors, angles, or uses (e.g., t-shirt flat lay, mug on desk, planner in hands).

Product Categories to Showcase

- Apparel (shirts, hoodies, tote bags)

- Stationery (notebooks, stickers, planners)

- Home items (mugs, coasters, pillows)

- Digital items (screens, device mockups)

A well-crafted product mockup project communicates your market-readiness, especially if you plan to work with digital merchants or design for independent creators.

Concept Posters Using Layer Stacking

Posters are where graphic designers get to show both technical and imaginative range. The most compelling posters use visual metaphor, layered compositions, and deliberate negative space. This project puts your composition and creativity under the spotlight.

Purpose

This project demonstrates:

- Conceptual thinking

- Layer stacking and masking expertise

- Typography integration

- Contrast and hierarchy management

How to Construct a Concept Poster

Step 1: Choose a subject or theme
This could be a film idea, event, book title, or abstract concept (like "Time," "Noise," "Solitude").

Step 2: Collect supporting imagery
Use a blend of stock textures, portraits, shapes, and symbols. Ensure all are license-free or your own captures.

Step 3: Stack elements deliberately
Use layers to build dimension. Cut out your subject, place abstract textures or paint splashes behind them, then insert fine details (smoke, particles, streaks) on top.

Step 4: Use masks—not erasers
Layer masks let you reveal or hide parts of layers cleanly and reversibly. Brush in gradual fades or sharp edges where needed.

Step 5: Integrate typography
Keep fonts bold and minimal. Use contrast to separate the headline from secondary text. Align to image features (like eyes, edges, or axis lines).

Step 6: Apply final color grading
Use **Gradient Maps**, **Selective Color**, or **Color Lookup Tables (LUTs)** to unify the palette.

Poster Composition Guidelines

- Don't crowd the center—offset focal points

- Limit to 2–3 fonts maximum

- Stick with one dominant color tone and one accent

- Always check poster readability at thumbnail size

This type of project shows your range—from commercial design to art direction.

Part IV
Advanced Workflows &
Automation

Chapter 11

Custom Presets, Actions, and Batch Editing

Consistency in digital editing is not only a matter of aesthetics—it's a mark of professionalism. Whether working on a set of product photos or retouching a client's portrait session, repeating the same steps manually can become tedious and time-consuming. This is where automation features like presets, recorded actions, and batch scripts come in. When used effectively, these tools not only increase your output speed but also help maintain quality across dozens—or even hundreds—of files.

This chapter explores practical ways to build and apply presets, record reusable actions, and perform batch operations without compromising the originality or quality of your work. Whether you're editing family photos, e-commerce assets, or creative art projects, these strategies will help streamline your workflow while keeping your creative fingerprint intact.

Setting Up Presets for Repetitive Tasks

Presets are predefined adjustments or filters saved for reuse. Unlike one-size-fits-all templates, well-made presets are flexible enough to speed up your work while still allowing space for personal tweaks.

What Presets Can Control

Presets can store combinations of:

- Color balance adjustments

- Tone curves

- Contrast and exposure levels

- Sharpening and clarity settings

- HSL (Hue, Saturation, Luminance) modifications

- Vignette and grain levels

Practical Uses of Custom Presets

1. Product Photography
If you regularly photograph items against a white or light grey background, you can create a preset that boosts clarity, reduces shadows, and corrects white balance without needing to re-adjust for each shoot.

2. Portrait Sessions
Save a soft skin-tone preset with gentle contrast and warm tones for multiple portraits taken under similar lighting.

3. Document Scanning or Flat Art
Create a preset that lifts shadows, reduces noise, and applies a subtle sharpening pass—ideal for consistent reproduction of paper-based work.

How to Create and Save Your Own Presets

Step 1: Edit a base photo manually
Apply all desired tone, contrast, and color corrections. Make sure your choices are adaptable across similar photos.

Step 2: Save the configuration
 Depending on your editing software, there will be an option to **"Save Preset,"** **"Create New Look,"** or **"Store Settings"**—use a descriptive title (e.g., "Soft Portrait - Warm 01").

Step 3: Apply with review, not blind automation
 Even though presets save time, always double-check how each one looks when applied to a new image. Lighting shifts, skin tone differences, or camera changes can affect results.

Creating and Recording Actions in Elements

Actions are recorded sequences of editing steps that can be played back with a single click. They're incredibly useful when applying the same process repeatedly—like resizing, applying filters, or exporting in a certain format.

What Can Be Recorded in an Action

- Layer creation and renaming

- Filter applications (blur, sharpen, etc.)

- Image adjustments (brightness, hue, levels)

- Merging and flattening layers

- Export operations

Steps to Record an Action (Compatible Editors)

Step 1: Open an image and go to the Actions or Automation Panel
 Look for a tab labeled "Actions," "Automation," or similar, depending on your software.

Step 2: Create a new action

Click "New Action" and give it a clear name. This allows easy retrieval later. Avoid generic titles like "Test 1" or "Filter Action."

Step 3: Start recording

Click the Record button and begin your workflow. Every tool you select, every layer you adjust, and every filter you apply will be saved in sequence.

Step 4: Stop when finished

Click "Stop Recording" when you're done. You now have a custom action saved in your library.

Step 5: Test it on a new file

Apply the action to a different image to ensure that all steps execute correctly without errors or unexpected results.

Tips for Building Better Actions

- Avoid including image-specific selections (like manually cropping a face)

- Keep naming conventions clean so others—or your future self—can understand what the action does

- If you're resizing or exporting, work on duplicates to avoid overwriting originals

---

Batch Resizing, Watermarking, and Auto-Touch-Up Scripts

Batch processing means applying a function or group of steps to multiple files at once. This is especially helpful for photographers, product sellers, or digital artists who need to prepare large sets of files with uniform requirements.

Batch Resizing

Ideal for:

- Web optimization

- Social media publishing

- Email sharing

- Archiving or thumbnails

Steps to Batch Resize

1. Create a folder containing all images to resize

2. Open the batch or automation tool in your editor

3. Choose the resize action or create a new one

4. Define the dimensions (e.g., width: 1500px, height: auto)

5. Set your output location and naming rule

6. Start the batch process

Note: Always keep the aspect ratio locked unless you're working with standard formats (e.g., product grids or ID photo sizes).

Batch Watermarking

Watermarks help prevent unauthorized use and communicate branding. Whether it's a discreet logo in the corner or a faint overlay, batch watermarking ensures consistency.

Steps to Apply Watermarks in Batches

1. Prepare your watermark file as a PNG with a transparent background

2. Record an action that imports, resizes, positions, and sets opacity for the watermark

3. Use the batch processor to apply this action to an entire folder

4. Export with unique names to avoid confusion with originals

Watermark Best Practices

- Use subtle transparency (around 40–60%)

- Avoid putting watermarks dead-center unless necessary

- Maintain consistent placement (e.g., bottom-right corner, 50px margin)

Auto-Touch-Up Scripts

Automated touch-ups can include:

- Basic skin smoothing

- Sharpening edges

- Adjusting lighting

- Fixing slight color imbalances

These scripts are best when used on consistent sets, such as product photos under studio lighting or passport photos under identical conditions.

Scripting vs. Recording:

While actions record what you *do*, scripts allow conditional logic (e.g., "if image width > 2000px, resize; else skip resizing"). You can create simple scripts using built-in editors or install script plugins compatible with your platform.

Keeping Things Organized

Creating custom tools only works when your workflow is clean. Here's how to avoid confusion and file loss.

Folder Naming

Use naming formats like:

- `ClientName_Project_Date`

- `PresetLibrary_Color_Muted`

- `ActionPack_Basics_2025`

Backing Up Presets and Actions

Always export your presets and action files periodically. Save backups both locally and on cloud storage. If your editing software ever crashes or updates, you'll have your workflow tools ready to reinstall.

Chapter 12

Color Grading Like a Filmmaker

Color grading is not just an aesthetic choice—it's a storytelling tool. Every shade, highlight, and contrast decision shapes the mood and guides how viewers interpret the image. While the technique is often associated with video editing, many of the same concepts apply powerfully to still photography. Whether you're refining portraits, conceptual art, or promotional material, understanding how to apply cinematic color grading will elevate your work far beyond the basics of brightness and contrast.

This chapter walks you through how to apply color grading in a photographic environment using software with lookup table (LUT) support, as well as manual grading techniques inspired by cinematic color language. You'll also learn how to craft and save your own grading styles that can be applied consistently across multiple projects.

Color Lookup Tables (LUTs) in Elements

What Are LUTs?

A LUT (short for *Look-Up Table*) is a file that translates colors from one range to another. It functions like a sophisticated preset for color and tone mapping. Unlike basic filters, LUTs work by referencing a mathematical formula to apply targeted changes across highlights, midtones, and shadows simultaneously.

How LUTs Work in Photo Editors

When you apply a LUT in your editing software, you're essentially overlaying a color model onto your image. This process changes the image's color profile to reflect a specific atmosphere or visual tone—without permanently altering the original pixels unless flattened.

Common LUT Formats

- **.CUBE** – One of the most widely supported LUT formats

- **.3DL** – Used in some pro-level color grading tools

- **.LOOK** – Found in certain specialized suites, not recommended for general compatibility

Where to Source Free and Legal LUTs

Make sure to download LUTs from platforms that offer open-use files. Reliable sources include public domain archives, educator-led repositories, or file-sharing sites that specify open licensing. Never use LUTs embedded in commercial software unless you own a license that allows redistribution or export.

How to Apply LUTs in Common Editors

Step 1: Add an Adjustment Layer
Select an option like "Color Lookup" or "Apply LUT" depending on your software.

Step 2: Load Your LUT File
Click to browse for a .CUBE file and apply it. Your image will instantly adopt the new color palette.

Step 3: Adjust Opacity or Blend Mode
Tone down the effect using layer opacity, or use blend modes like "Soft Light" or "Color" to mix it more subtly into the image.

Step 4: Mask If Needed

Apply a layer mask to restrict the LUT effect to specific areas, like backgrounds or clothing, while preserving skin tone accuracy.

Cinematic Grading Techniques

While LUTs are a powerful shortcut, learning to manually adjust color settings gives you greater flexibility and control. This is especially important when your image requires a more tailored emotional tone or when working with mixed lighting conditions.

Color Psychology and Storytelling

Color grading, at its core, is about guiding emotional response.

- **Cool tones (blue, teal, cyan)** create calm, isolation, or suspense

- **Warm tones (orange, gold, red)** evoke energy, intimacy, or nostalgia

- **Desaturated tones** often suggest realism, seriousness, or vintage appeal

- **High contrast grading** builds visual tension or dramatic intensity

Understanding how these tones work in conjunction with your subject matter is crucial.

Basic Grading Layers to Work With

- **Exposure and Contrast** – Set the mood with light intensity differences

- **Curves and Levels** – Fine-tune highlights, midtones, and shadows independently

- **Color Balance** – Shift tones within shadows, midtones, and highlights

- **Selective Color** – Modify individual color ranges (reds, blues, greens, etc.)

- **Gradient Maps** – Replace tonal ranges with preset gradients for abstract or stylized results

Building a Film-Like Grade from Scratch

Step 1: Set Exposure and Base Contrast
Correct any overexposure or underexposure. Establish a gentle S-curve using the curves adjustment layer to increase depth without harsh edges.

Step 2: Adjust Color Balance
Introduce cinematic undertones: blues into shadows, oranges into highlights. Be subtle—minor shifts are more believable.

Step 3: Selective Desaturation
Lower the saturation on less important elements (like background foliage) to direct focus toward skin or focal objects.

Step 4: Add a Gradient Overlay (Optional)
Use a gradient to darken the top and bottom edges (vignette effect) and direct the viewer's eye to the center. Blend this using low opacity and soft light mode.

Step 5: Save Before Flattening
Always save your graded version in a format that preserves layers (like PSD) before exporting for web or print.

Creating Your Own Look Presets

Once you've perfected a grade that fits your visual style, saving it as a reusable preset allows you to apply it quickly to other projects without starting from scratch each time.

How to Save Custom Looks

1. Organize Your Layers

Group all grading-related layers into a folder. Name it clearly, such as "Vintage Cool – Soft Contrast."

2. Export as a Template or Adjustment File

Depending on your software, you can export the entire adjustment stack as a reusable file. If presets aren't supported, save a duplicate file as a working template and replace the photo layer when reusing.

3. Test Your Preset on Multiple Images

Apply the preset to various types of photos—indoor, outdoor, low light—to ensure flexibility.

4. Refine and Version Your Presets

If your look works better on bright portraits than on moody still lifes, create two versions: "Bright – Cool 01" and "Moody – Cool 01."

Tips for Better Grading Presets

- Avoid extreme curve adjustments—leave room for future tweaks

- Don't rely on filters that permanently alter pixels; always work non-destructively

- Make notes on what your preset does and what kind of image it's designed for

Key Considerations for Visual Consistency

1. Match Lighting Across Sets

Before applying any color grade, make sure the base lighting across a series of photos is relatively consistent. Color grading can't fix inconsistent lighting—it only amplifies it.

2. Calibrate Your Monitor
Editing with an uncalibrated screen means your color grading decisions may appear differently on other devices or prints.

3. Save Variants for Social Media, Print, and Web
What looks rich and vibrant on a print might appear oversaturated on a phone. Always preview your graded image in different color profiles (sRGB for web, CMYK for print).

Chapter 13

Advanced Selections, Channels, and Blend Strategies

Precision is what separates a decent image from a powerful one. In image editing, particularly when dealing with complex composites, fine selections and blend strategies become non-negotiable. This chapter covers how to work with challenging elements like hair, glass, and semi-transparent materials, use blending modes with targeted intent, and manipulate channels for intricate compositing. Whether you're isolating a subject from a chaotic background or merging layers with subtle realism, these advanced tools give you the upper hand.

Hair Selections, Glass, and Translucent Objects

Why These Elements Are Difficult

Hair strands, frosted glass, smoke, fabric, and similar textures share one problem: their edges are irregular, often partially see-through, and lack high contrast against the background. This makes them difficult to isolate with basic lasso tools or rectangular selections. Fortunately, there are techniques specifically designed to handle these complexities.

Techniques for Isolating Hair

1. Use a High-Contrast Background
When possible, start with an image that features strong contrast between the

subject's hair and the background. The more separation in brightness or color, the easier the extraction.

2. Convert to a Channel-Based Mask

Inspect the red, green, and blue channels individually (via the Channels panel). Look for the one that provides the clearest contrast between the hair and the background.

- Duplicate the best channel.

- Increase the contrast using levels or curves.

- Use the Brush tool to clean the mask by painting black or white manually.

- Convert this into a selection by holding Ctrl (or Command) and clicking the channel thumbnail.

3. Refine with Select and Mask Tools

Once a rough selection is made, use a Refine Edge or similar tool. Focus on enabling "Smart Radius" or equivalent features that dynamically detect edge textures like hair.

4. Layer Mask for Non-Destructive Editing

Always apply your selection as a layer mask. This allows for later cleanup without affecting the original pixels.

Handling Glass and Semi-Transparent Surfaces

Glass objects require a unique approach since they reflect and refract background elements. These aren't always separable through simple edge detection.

Steps to Approach Translucency:

- Lower the opacity of the layer with the glass object and observe the interplay between layers.

- Use a soft-edged mask to control transparency gradation.

- Consider duplicating the layer, applying different blend modes (e.g., Screen for highlights), and masking areas selectively.

- Adjust hue and saturation independently to better match the composite lighting.

Using Blend Modes with Purpose

Blend modes are often underutilized because many users experiment without understanding their specific function. Each mode is a mathematical formula that instructs how two layers interact. Knowing how to use them with intent—rather than trial and error—saves time and produces more believable results.

Key Blend Modes and When to Use Them

Multiply

- **Effect:** Darkens the base layer according to the blend layer

- **Best For:** Adding shadows, darkening skies, reinforcing ink or texture overlays

Screen

- **Effect:** Lightens the base layer by inverting, multiplying, and inverting again

- **Best For:** Brightening subjects, glow effects, soft light simulations

Overlay

- **Effect:** Combines Multiply and Screen depending on the base layer brightness

- **Best For:** Enhancing contrast, boosting texture, or stylizing portraits

Soft Light

- **Effect:** A subtler version of Overlay, with more nuance in midtones

- **Best For:** Natural light effects, facial highlights, gentle glow

Color

- **Effect:** Applies the hue and saturation of the top layer while preserving luminosity

- **Best For:** Toning work without affecting contrast, changing color mood

Luminosity

- **Effect:** Applies the brightness values of the top layer, ignoring its hue/saturation

- **Best For:** Correcting highlights or shadows without altering color

Tips for Clean Blending

- **Never apply blend modes to the entire image blindly**
  Use masks to isolate the effect to specific areas.

- **Always review on different backgrounds**
  What looks good on white may not hold up on dark or textured scenes.

- **Use neutral gray when building dodge/burn layers**
  A 50% gray layer set to Soft Light makes a flexible, non-destructive way to

brighten or darken specific spots.

Multi-Channel Compositing Techniques

Beyond the visible layers, image editors use channels—separated into red, green, and blue—to define tonal information. These channels can be exploited for powerful selection building, mask refinement, and even special effects.

Understanding the Channel Structure

Each image channel stores grayscale information about one part of the color spectrum:

- **Red channel:** Often shows good contrast in skin tones

- **Green channel:** Typically the sharpest and most detailed

- **Blue channel:** Contains more noise and is usually darkest

Isolating Detail Through Channels

Step 1: Evaluate Channels Separately
Look at each channel to find where the contrast between subject and background is strongest. This often depends on the image type—portraits may favor red, while outdoor scenes may lean toward green.

Step 2: Duplicate the Best Channel
Create a copy of the most useful channel to preserve the original.

Step 3: Enhance Separation
Use Levels, Curves, or Burn/Dodge tools to exaggerate contrast.

Step 4: Create a Layer Mask from the Channel
Once you're satisfied, convert this into a selection and apply it as a mask on the target layer.

Combining Multiple Channels for Special Effects

You can recombine channels in unexpected ways to generate creative results:

- **Replace one channel with another for stylistic shifts**
  For instance, swap the red and green channels for an infrared-style look.

- **Overlay a channel as a texture**
  The green channel, due to its detail, can serve as a base for sharpening or texture maps.

- **Use Channel Calculations (in compatible editors)**
  Some software allows you to blend two channels together mathematically (Add, Subtract, Multiply) to generate complex masks or tonal effects.

Practical Application Scenarios

Isolating a Person from a Busy Background

1. Use channel-based masking for hair.

2. Refine with selective masking and soft brushes.

3. Adjust tones using blend modes like Soft Light for contouring.

4. Clean up edges by feathering the mask slightly or using defringe options.

Adding a Glass Object into a Scene

1. Place the object on a new layer.

2. Lower its opacity to 60–70% to simulate light behavior.

3. Duplicate the object layer.

4. Set the top layer to Screen mode and mask only highlight areas.

5. Adjust background blur behind the glass to match depth perception.

Part V
The Professional Edge

Chapter 14

Working with Clients and Deliverables

Working with clients extends beyond the creative phase—it involves technical precision, reliable delivery practices, and the ability to communicate clearly under tight deadlines. Even the most visually compelling design work loses credibility if it's delivered in the wrong size, color format, or resolution. This chapter equips you with the knowledge to prepare files for commercial printing, understand technical export settings, and organize deliverables like a professional—leaving no room for misunderstandings or costly revisions.

Preparing Print-Ready Files: Bleed, CMYK, and Sizing

What Makes a File "Print-Ready"?

A print-ready file is more than just a high-resolution image. It must meet specific requirements that allow a commercial printer to reproduce your design without surprises. This includes accurate sizing, color management, and allowance for trimming.

Bleed and Trim Zones

What Is Bleed?
Bleed is the area that extends beyond the final trim size of your document. It exists

to ensure that when the paper is cut to size, there are no unwanted white edges—even if the trim is slightly off.

- **Standard Bleed Size:** Most commercial printers request a bleed of 0.125 inches (or 3 mm) on all sides.

- **How to Add It:** Extend background elements or imagery beyond the final page size by the required amount.

- **Trim Line vs. Safe Zone:**

  - The **trim line** is the intended final size.

  - The **safe zone** is the area inside the trim line where all essential text and graphics should stay, typically 0.125"–0.25" inside the trim.

CMYK vs. RGB

Why It Matters:

Commercial printers work with CMYK (Cyan, Magenta, Yellow, and Key/Black) inks. If your file is in RGB (Red, Green, Blue), it must be converted—either by you or by the printer. Relying on the printer to convert it often leads to color shifts and surprises.

Steps to Convert Safely:

1. Set your document color mode to CMYK before beginning the design (when possible).

2. If you're working with images or assets in RGB, convert them manually using color profile settings.

3. Use soft proofing to simulate how your colors will appear in print.

Resizing Without Losing Quality

How to Resize for Print:

- Use vector-based formats for logos and text-heavy graphics.

- For raster files (like photos), always start with the highest resolution available.

- Avoid upscaling small images, as this will degrade quality and introduce visible pixels or artifacts.

Standard Print Sizes (U.S. Examples):

- Business Cards: 3.5 x 2 inches + bleed

- Letterhead: 8.5 x 11 inches + bleed

- Posters: 11 x 17, 18 x 24, or 24 x 36 inches

Understanding DPI, Resolution, and Export Formats

DPI vs. PPI: Know the Difference

These terms are often confused, but they refer to different stages in the output process.

- **PPI (Pixels Per Inch):** Refers to the pixel density of a digital image.

- **DPI (Dots Per Inch):** Refers to the physical dot density a printer uses.

Standard Settings:

- **Print:** 300 PPI (recommended)

- **Web:** 72–96 PPI

Why It Matters:

Sending a client or printer a 72 PPI image for print will result in a blurry, low-quality output—even if it looks fine on screen.

Resolution Tips for Print Projects

- **Check actual image dimensions in inches or millimeters** when setting resolution.

- When designing at 300 PPI, a 6 x 4 inch file should be at least 1800 x 1200 pixels.

- **Use "Image Size" and not "Canvas Size"** when resizing for resolution without affecting visible area.

Choosing the Right File Format

Different clients and printing companies may ask for specific formats depending on their systems. Here's a breakdown of common types and their purpose:

Format	Best Use Case	Notes
PDF	Universal print delivery	Flatten layers, embed fonts, preserve vector elements
TIFF	High-res photo printing	Uncompressed; large file sizes
EPS	Vector printing (logos)	Use for scalable graphics
JPEG	Web previews or low-priority prints	Compresses image; quality may drop

| PNG | Digital use with transparency | Not ideal for print due to RGB color space |

How to Package and Deliver Files Like a Pro

When delivering final work, your organization and communication matter just as much as the content itself. Clients—especially those unfamiliar with design software—appreciate clarity, options, and confidence in your preparation.

Organizing Final Files

Create a clean folder structure before delivering anything:

markdown

```
/ProjectName-FinalFiles
   /Print
       - BusinessCard_Final_CMYK.pdf
       - Poster_24x36_TIFF.tif
   /Web
       - Banner_RGB_Web.jpg
   /SourceFiles
       - ProjectFile.psd or .ai
       - Fonts (if allowed)
       - Linked Images
   /ReadMe
       - Instructions or usage notes
```

Label clearly: Avoid naming files "final_version_2_revised_v3_flattened.psd". Use clean, dated filenames that remove ambiguity.

Packaging for Print Production

Most design software offers a **Package** feature that collects all fonts, linked images, and assets into a single folder. Use this feature when sending layered files to a printing partner.

- Always **embed fonts** in PDFs if font licensing permits.

- Provide **both flattened and layered versions** in case edits are needed.

- Include a **print specs sheet** outlining:

    ○ Color mode (CMYK)

    ○ Resolution (300 PPI)

    ○ Trim size and bleed

    ○ Spot or Pantone colors if used

Delivering Files to Clients

Send Files Through Secure Platforms:
Use reliable file transfer tools that support large file sizes and provide download tracking, such as:

- Google Drive (with clear folder naming)

- Dropbox (with "View-only" links unless edit access is needed)

- WeTransfer or other link-based services for clients who aren't tech-savvy

Include a Delivery Checklist:

- Final exports in required formats (PDF, JPEG, etc.)

- Fonts (if legally allowed)

- Editable source files (PSD, AI)

- Print and web-ready versions

- ReadMe or instruction guide

- Proofs or mockups (optional but professional)

Tips for Communicating with Clients

- **Set Expectations Early:** Clarify whether you will provide layered files, printing assistance, or only export-ready files.

- **Always Confirm Specs Before Designing:** Ask for trim sizes, resolution requirements, color preferences, and acceptable file types upfront.

- **Avoid Sending Only One Format:** Even if the client asks for a JPEG, also send a PDF or layered file so they're covered in the future.

- **Document All Revisions:** Keep dated folders for version tracking to avoid confusion or disputes.

Chapter 15

Building a Side Hustle with Your Skills

Graphic design and digital artistry are not limited to agency work or client commissions. With consistent skill and a structured approach, you can turn your design proficiency into multiple income streams. Whether it's through selling digital products, freelancing, or licensing your work, there are clear methods for building an independent, profitable side income. This chapter lays out how to establish your side hustle strategically and responsibly.

Selling Templates, Presets, and Digital Art

Why Digital Products Are a Smart Choice

Digital products require a one-time investment of time and skill to create, but they can be sold repeatedly without the overhead of physical inventory. These products are attractive to small business owners, creators, and even other designers who want ready-made solutions.

Types of Digital Products You Can Sell

Templates

- **Presentation Templates:** Designed for platforms like PowerPoint or Keynote.

- **Social Media Kits:** Post layouts for platforms such as Instagram, Pinterest, and YouTube.

- **Business Collateral:** Brochure templates, invoices, business cards, and letterheads.

- **Resumés and Portfolios:** Pre-formatted documents with stylish, editable content sections.

Presets

- **Photo Editing Presets:** Color grading and lighting adjustments for photo-editing software.

- **Video LUTs:** For filmmakers or content creators who want stylized footage.

- **Typography Styles:** Custom effects or character settings for consistent brand visuals.

Digital Art

- **Printable Artworks:** Abstract pieces, typographic quotes, or illustrations.

- **Digital Wallpapers:** Designed for desktops, mobile, or tablets.

- **Icons and Graphic Packs:** Useful for UI/UX designers or app developers.

Platforms to Sell Your Work

Avoid trademarked marketplace names, but know that there are many open marketplace-style platforms and self-hosted options where designers sell digital goods legally and independently.

Examples of Distribution Methods:

- **Personal Website with Payment Integration**

- **Email-Based Direct Sales**

- **Open-source eCommerce platforms (like WooCommerce or Big Cartel)**

When setting up your store, always provide:

- A full product description

- Preview images

- Licensing details (personal use, commercial use, etc.)

- Clear download instructions

How to Make Your Products Stand Out

- Create products that solve a problem, not just look good.

- Include clear naming conventions in your files.

- Add bonus items (e.g., alternate color palettes, instructions, editable layers).

- Offer regular updates for evolving trends or software changes.

Freelancing for Small Businesses and Creators

Why Target Small Businesses?

Independent business owners often need branding, social media content, or marketing collateral but may not have in-house designers. They are often more flexible and open to forming long-term working relationships. This makes them ideal clients for consistent freelance income.

Services You Can Offer

- **Logo and Brand Design**

- **Social Media Content Creation**

- **Website Graphics or Banners**

- **Flyer and Poster Design**

- **Packaging Mockups**

- **Product Photography Retouching**

Where to Find Clients (Without Platform Name-Dropping)

- **Online Forums and Entrepreneur Groups**

- **Local Business Directories**

- **Industry-Specific Online Communities**

- **Your Own Portfolio Website or Blog**

When reaching out to clients:

- Be specific about how you can help them (e.g., "I help food trucks design eye-catching menus and signage").

- Always include a portfolio or sample gallery, even if you're just starting—use mock projects if needed.

Structuring Your Freelance Offers

Start by creating service packages to make decision-making easier for clients:

- **Basic Package:** 1 design, limited revisions, basic format delivery

- **Standard Package:** 2–3 designs, up to 3 revisions, layered files

- **Premium Package:** Multiple assets, full rights, and consulting

Always be clear about what is included and set expectations about turnaround times and licensing rights.

Licensing Your Work and Copyright Tips

Understanding Copyright Basics

Copyright protects original creative works the moment they are created. As the creator, you own the rights unless you explicitly transfer them in writing.

- You automatically hold copyright to all original graphics, illustrations, and designs you make.

- A client does not own the full rights to your work unless you license or sell those rights in a written agreement.

Types of Licensing

Personal Use License

The buyer may use the file for non-commercial purposes but cannot resell, modify, or redistribute it.

Commercial Use License

Allows the buyer to use the design in revenue-generating activities. This may include use in advertisements, packaging, or websites. You can further restrict it by:

- Number of prints or uses allowed

- Whether the design can be modified

- Whether attribution is required

Exclusive vs. Non-Exclusive

- **Exclusive License:** The buyer is the only person who may use the work in the defined manner.

- **Non-Exclusive License:** The same file can be sold to multiple people.

How to Protect Your Work

- Always watermark previews that are publicly shared.

- Include licensing documentation in your download folders.

- Keep track of who buys what by using invoices and logs.

- Use software to embed metadata into your images.

Drafting Simple Licensing Agreements

Even a one-page agreement can protect your rights. Include:

- Description of the work

- Scope of usage (where and how it may be used)

- Duration of the license

- Whether modifications are allowed

- Payment terms

- Signature and date

You don't need to use complex legal language—just be clear and direct.

Tips for Growing Your Side Hustle Sustainably

- **Track Your Time:** Know how long each task takes, so you can price accordingly.

- **Keep Records:** Maintain records of sales, licenses, and communications.

- **Separate Business and Personal Files:** Use folders and file-naming systems that reflect professional organization.

- **Keep Improving Your Skills:** Side hustles are competitive. Stay updated by learning new tools and techniques.

Appendices & Bonus Resources

These supplementary materials are crafted to support your ongoing learning and problem-solving as you continue building your skillset. From optimized workflow tips to legal clarity on media usage, each appendix provides concise, actionable knowledge that remains useful well beyond your first project.

Appendix A: Keyboard Shortcuts Cheat Sheet (2025 Edition)

Mastering keyboard shortcuts is a smart way to work faster and reduce unnecessary clicks. While some shortcuts are common across graphic software, others may be specific depending on your program of choice. Below are widely accepted keyboard commands categorized by function. These have been generalized for compatibility across major creative platforms, avoiding any brand-specific tool names.

General Workflow Shortcuts

Action	Shortcut (Windows)	Shortcut (macOS)
Save	Ctrl + S	Cmd + S
Save As	Ctrl + Shift + S	Cmd + Shift + S
Open	Ctrl + O	Cmd + O
New File	Ctrl + N	Cmd + N
Close Document	Ctrl + W	Cmd + W
Undo	Ctrl + Z	Cmd + Z
Redo	Ctrl + Shift + Z	Cmd + Shift + Z

Selection and Navigation

Action	Shortcut (Windows)	Shortcut (macOS)

Select All	Ctrl + A	Cmd + A
Deselect	Ctrl + D	Cmd + D
Zoom In	Ctrl + +	Cmd + +
Zoom Out	Ctrl + -	Cmd + -
Fit to Screen	Ctrl + 0	Cmd + 0
Hand Tool (Pan)	Spacebar	Spacebar

Layer and Object Controls

Action	Shortcut (Windows)	Shortcut (macOS)
Duplicate Layer/Object	Ctrl + J	Cmd + J
Bring Forward	Ctrl +]	Cmd +]
Send Backward	Ctrl + [	Cmd + [
Group	Ctrl + G	Cmd + G
Ungroup	Ctrl + Shift + G	Cmd + Shift + G
Lock Layer	Ctrl + /	Cmd + /

Note: These are generalized functions. Always refer to the specific documentation of the software you use for the most accurate results.

Appendix B: Free Online Assets and Brush Repositories

If you're just starting or building a self-funded project, free tools can significantly improve your work without compromising quality. Below are some of the most reliable open-license resources for designers.

Open License Image Resources

- **Pixabay** – Offers high-resolution photos and vector files with no attribution required.

- **Pexels** – Known for modern, editorial-style stock photography and video.

- **Unsplash** – Ideal for artistic and stylized images, usable without licensing restrictions.

Free Brush Libraries

- **Brusheezy** – A hub of user-contributed brushes and textures for multiple software environments.

- **DeviantArt Brush Packs** – Many creators share their brush presets under public licenses. Always double-check usage rights.

- **OpenBrushResources.org** – A curated list of high-quality, unrestricted-use brush collections.

Icons and Vector Files

- **SVGRepo** – Free scalable vector graphics for use in UI and branding.

- **HeroIcons (open variant)** – Clean, minimal icons you can freely modify.

When using these resources, verify the licensing terms on each download page. Avoid using anything labeled "editorial use only" for commercial projects.

Appendix C: Troubleshooting Guide for Crashes, Lag, and Errors

Every designer encounters technical glitches. Instead of starting over or wasting time restarting your software repeatedly, use the guide below to resolve common issues swiftly.

Crashes on Launch

- **Check Hardware Compatibility:** Make sure your computer meets the minimum processor and memory requirements for the software.

- **Update Graphics Drivers:** Crashes often happen due to outdated GPU drivers.

- **Clear Temporary Files:** Temporary caches may corrupt over time. Clearing them often resolves startup crashes.

Sluggish Performance or Lag

- **Lower Undo History Count:** Reducing the number of history states conserves memory.

- **Decrease Canvas Size:** Large, high-resolution files slow down even powerful machines.

- **Limit Active Layers:** Try merging or flattening unused layers to reduce processing strain.

- **Allocate More RAM (if supported):** Some programs allow you to increase the memory available.

Freezes When Exporting

- **Use Export Queues Instead of Quick Export:** This spreads processing over time and minimizes overload.

- **Avoid High Bit Depth Unless Required:** 16-bit or 32-bit color depth may be excessive unless specifically requested by a client.

- **Save Locally, Not to Cloud Drives:** External sync folders may slow down or interrupt saving processes.

Appendix D: Legal Use of Stock Images and AI-Generated Content

Using external media in your designs adds richness and saves time, but it comes with responsibilities. Understanding the rules avoids the risk of takedowns, lawsuits, or rejection from online marketplaces.

Stock Image Usage Rules

- **Always Read the License:** Just because an image is labeled as "free" does not mean it's suitable for commercial use.

- **Avoid Editorial-Only Images:** These are typically only for news articles and cannot be used in business projects.

- **Do Not Resell or Repackage:** Stock files should not be distributed as-is. Your design must modify or integrate the asset creatively.

AI-Generated Content Guidelines

AI-generated art introduces unique legal questions. While no global standard currently exists, certain principles help you stay safe:

- **Do Not Claim Exclusive Ownership:** AI tools do not qualify you for full intellectual property protection in many regions.

- **Avoid Faces and Recognizable Places:** Many models are trained on public figures or real-world imagery, which could trigger likeness rights claims.

- **Use AI Work as a Component, Not the Whole:** Always apply your own design decisions on top—layout, editing, text, or combined assets.

When publishing, include a note that any AI-generated portions were modified, supervised, and integrated by you to create a final original product.

Appendix E: How to Stay Updated Without Relearning Everything

Digital tools change often, but that doesn't mean you need to start from scratch every year. Keeping up with your software, trends, and industry norms can be structured around habits, not panic.

Use Official Product Documentation

Most software makers maintain detailed, public manuals and update logs. Set a reminder to review these quarterly. Focus only on the tools you regularly use.

Subscribe to Non-Commercial Learning Platforms

Instead of marketplace blogs that push branded tools, follow technical blogs, public newsletters, or independent designers who focus on practical use rather than promotion.

Watch Software Update Videos

Some communities release short-format videos summarizing changes in tools or workflows. Choose ones that are under 10 minutes and skip anything that is overly branded or clickbait-driven.

Don't Update Mid-Project

Always wait until you've completed a project before switching to a newer version of your tool. Update in your downtime and allow space for testing before relying on it for client work.

Keep a "What Changed" Log

Maintain a personal document noting what changes affected your workflow after each update. This keeps the learning process lightweight and personalized, with no need to rely on memory.